*To and From
on the
Day-for-Night
Coast*

To and From on the Day-for-Night Coast

a time mobius

stephen francis cosgrove

REGENT PRESS
Berkeley, California
2017

Copyright © 2017 by Steve Cosgrove

ISBN 13: 978-1-58790-406-6
ISBN 10: 1-58790-406-3
Library of Congress Control Number: forthcoming

To contact the author:
cozzy2424@gmail.com

Manufactured in the U.S.A.
REGENT PRESS
Berkeley, California
www.regentpress.net

preface

I came to words via music, having enjoyed many years studying Mozart and Chopin. In San Francisco I was drawn to the readings and was lucky to hear some of the Old Spaghetti Factory series and later Cafe Babar. So many great evenings! But I always thought it would be cool to have a poetry reading at 7:30 am as well, somewhere. No one agreed.

Anyway, I thought I'd write a book. Literally, write it. This is the result. I'm not inclined to explain it. Some of what's in these pages happened. Some things did not. Like the reference to LSD on page 71. The line just happened.

As for the title, it was a road trip. The cops show up several times in the text. Its because I speed and I like to know where they are.

The "day for night" has to do with how night scenes used to be filmed. In the day time. But none of us were really fooled and I know you won't be fooled by this book either. What is entirely sincere however is my love for those to whom it is dedicated.

Stephen Francis Cosgrove

DEDICATION

*for
Harry
Helen
Jocelyn
and Karl*

TO-AND-FROM ON THE DAY-FOR-NIGHT COAST

Go see Harry   by day and night

Go getting day and night mixt
    So that it's fifties and sixties cinema you see

And say to those imaginary companions who accompany
    "Hey! let's get naked and make a mess!"
For it's only lucid dreaming done
    and as long as we stay on the road
        there's no harm   no harm at all

The cops will see it our way
Past Petaluma   Cotati
    with Penngrove somewhere

They're always constructing
They just can't help it!
Implementing business   business everywhere
    at a quarter-to-twelve

The date?
That's easy   a calendar's count in November
A fourteenth day in a thirteenth year
Passing all the places we knew and loved
    as state college staff
        when we'd say the Indian word "Sonoma"
        and hear them drumming to our academia

Santa Rosa tells no lies
    in the time it takes to roll on through
    101 a simplicity bisecting the town
        so that it's east and west on your way

The time? 11:45 a.m.
And the date?   that is known as well
    two-thirds into November
            day 14
            year 13

To get to Harry an extra day will be needed
Another teen of tenacious adolescence

Each evergreen is sentry to the roadwork
There has never been a time
    when the highway wasn't widening
Saint Rose!
  the Saintly Rose perfuming construction

Repeat the words "passing through"
  the places that meant so much
    whose meaning now is Nostalgia's question:
    can I remember and stay constructed
        myself?

Saying goodbye
Or rather remembering a goodbye said
       affectionately

Thinking "Adieu!" to be inadequate

She was elegant and tall and deserving of more
Deserving of a road trip herself
  when we might have counted together
      the lanes and miles
     just anything worthy of a list

There was a boss deceived told I wasn't well
For the truth was
  an extra day was needed to get all the way to Harry

"I have a pain
  I can't come in
   it's a headache
    might be the flu
     Sorry to bail!"

It was a story told well
But I needn't have worried
My colleagues called in sick so often
  in contrast to me
    I was more than excused

"Take as much time as you need
        no doctor's note's required!"

It felt good knowing the entire route would be leisurely
The only way it should be done
Anticipating Harry   glad I'd be seeing him
101 the freeway a promise narrower roads awaited
        were to come
          if you're careful through the corridor

I was prepared to accept
        even the building of a valley away
      if it meant the planet is saved for future Mozarts
    for entirely effective government
Perhaps a worldwide Windsor
        based on that town's layout

Strategic Peets
The coffee whose shop is almost enough
So aromatic is the inside space
    an actual purchase is moot
You read and learn
        while the scent of the bean alone satisfies

Suspended belief
    where caffeine stays a dormant addiction
           the olfactory sufficing

Having seen only .02% of the town of Windsor
    there was a rage to see the rest
But I needed the cooler clouds of the dampening coast
The baby-blue of new beginnings
    and whatever parents are left
        please continue protecting your son!

Asked that sheriff, "My friend?"
    (was I overly familiar?
    would he think his questioner
          a law enforcement groupie
          out to make conversation,
              any?)

"My friend?
    if you get a ticket on a res
        say, the Pyramid Lake Indian Reservation
        is that violation likely
            to make its way to California's DMV?"
He considered   wondered himself
                before saying, "Unlikely"

"Well, if you think so   so will I!"

We also agreed together
That it was extremely unlikely
        any crime was in progress in Windsor
And it seemed   fleetingly
        that the officer might turn too mild-mannered
                because of this

Windsor   an English California
Beyond whose city limits all was informal once more
    and dangerous

Between Cobb Mountain
            with its single lonely building
And the castle edifice of Saint Helena
    the summit eye ping-pongs
        to a radio's Republican screed about Obama
His health care
Your keeping or not keeping your health care plan
The voice earnest as forced ascents
    while suffering arteries to clog
                and harden with resentment
"Vote with the Republicans for a real fix!"

Yeah? which ones?
The Establishment ones?
Really?
You sure, radio?

The sum of nine hundred million is heard
Dollars? chipmunks? sparrows? which?
The pine needles spread in those mountains

                              and plucked as souvenirs?

Politics hatched in the landscape's early afternoon
And politics forces an emergency exit
     to accommodate the narcolepsy induced

That mountain   Cobb
Drive it in the mind
          the mind's maps open with first usage
            creases corresponding
                to the brain's crennelations
Such a neat packet of instructions!
The mountain's five thousand feet
     enough overlook to oversee the grapes

Being east of Cloverdale
Being teased by the sign that says "Citrus Fair"
Being aware of great heights and great depths
          you went slower
               passed by every driver

It is melancholy's islands joined
     and seeing houses others own
       a clairvoyance to the viewing
As if with a little effort
          every Cloverdale dweller may be known
who's just married
who's about to call it quits

I wish you'd have come
     this Dvorak's for both of us   truly
       the composer who could compose
          even in the midst of his family's noise
He would have the two of us together   he *would*
Just listen to *any* of his music! you'd see!
     you'd hear
       a violin concerto taking action
               on behalf of Czechoslovakia

Oh, wait!
     that's the Czech Republic and Slovakia now

                the splinters
Well, whatever borders he knew
                        he is borderless in sound
Sounding the high notes
The same as a bird in a lofty major key

Freeway with a blue barn   fleeting
Like an instant hostel provided by a farm
You're tired   you bed down   a creature of the hay

Or it's the sky's dormitory the high hills enclose
Thus many feet above the sea you feel better
        four-leaf   lucky
            in a field how few will be not found

I see the black-and-white version of a dream
And the sunshine in the valley is therefore white
        dualism's light
        the planet turning every shade
                without a spectrum's assistance

It takes no time at all to join a.m. and p.m.
                        money in the union

Let the clover instruct leaking green into the charcoal
I'm "drawing" my way
        to the Big Gibraltar north of town

Perhaps a Hater's Leap and not a Lover's
        Someone mad enough to do it
            and foreswear the madrone   the pine
                                        the details
Go for the big picture of death up there
Get used to it
    so that there's inevitability

Anger stepping out into sovereign space
State of ironic weightlessness
        and then   just a lack of information
The orange   the yellow lichen   baby ideas
First thoughts in the next life
        where there may or may not be baseball

         the way you like it   close
     with extra
             incomprehensible innings

A drop-off   there to convince us
               a wall may be tall, vertical
               despite the setting of hills
                   worn accessible
The miles out of Cloverdale
Like sudden calculations aided by topography
                              all of it safe

Don't be mad
Don't get mad
     unless it's the mad that Harry had to be
                         to beat the Germans

Comes the town that is capital "H" something
Before it is reached through the river's lands
      the rest of the town's name not coming
          the name   the name

Only the "H" is certain spelling
Certain as the beauty of that landmarking peak
                   south
                sure to have a name itself
                capital something
                           no doubt

The bridge   another green one
     whispers Washington State
         is just a matter of girders
             the Toutle traversed perhaps
There's so much green in that direction!
Green River Gorge   one of the greens

This town, though
Can you think of it   still shy of it?

Hopland!
That's its!
Yes, Hopland is remembered

before the city limit says it

The trees are questions
    now it's fall and the leaves no longer satisfy

"H" the History Channel
    has and will have no answers this year
We'll just have to settle for cannons
And hope the ammo's forthcoming
        that may blast some meaning

First the bridge though and what it spans
First talk about the braiding and meanders
And how misdirection's close enough
        for a river's jazz
This one crossed in sight of all good things
    and the hops that summarize
    and make them possible

And that mountain south of town
    is south of time   and timeout, too
It will take another day in another year
        to be tutored by the locals

Enter panorama, be part of its scrim
We can get all of Hopland back if we're clever
with delight and screaming silently
        so Hopland's not alarmed

I believe it's another dimension
        announced by trumpets
Let them sound almighty alternate countrysides!

Did I say, "panorama"?
Know there was lumber lain
    a flea market collectibles

Lakeville only nineteen miles east
    where once a mistic poetry reading was
Something driven to as now

Remember there was winding and danger

The passengers were two friends   one a ballet teacher
And we partied that night
    to the prologue to a poem simply "Ocean" called

Performance art informed by a lake
    with the volcano Kenocti at hand
        and we'd returned overtired
            from its virtual rumblings

Pan the Bocce Ball with hand-held gadgetry
    restaurant and tasting room
    the alcoholic will slide
If it's living right   it comes at too high a price
Events Center
    "Lost in Space" to be reenacted

Don't think
A dream is in charge
    Infusing Hopland with otherness and retro
Give me your hand   your ghostly hand
And I will walk your imaginary self
        to that Mini-Mart there
        anything you desire
        let's across the highway
            shall we?

Both of the numbers are prime
Prime Seven   prime Eleven
        the Eleven somehow more so

There's an eighteen wheeler waiting on a driver
"So far and no farther!" he'd said
    and then walked to Brutocalle
        passing under the delicate arch
            whitely built

The Italians are converging

And that southern mountain!
It's like one of their daily words
        filled with clarity
How long has "bocce" been a word?
Well there's plenty of parking

so much in fact that no one's home   or even at work
                              one and the same in this case

Travelling's a career that only the traveler knows
And these visitations so secretly promote
                         that advancement's assured
Kopland's playing Bocce Ball
Breaking the rules to please the tourist
Entertainment conceived by Leonardo da Vinci

Pull in also   if you like and doze
     and wait for employees to put yourself to work
I'd wake up they tap the window I'd be ready

In a yellow dawn
      will a peach-fuzz fog enhalo the oak trees
            made a Louisiana bayou
                   with abundant moss?
It is the beginning of the alligator's hour
A southern storm rising up
     beside the vineyards
     in their rusty state of autumn
          burnt umber encoring the season

You should be mine   left and right
                         as remnant vintage
The color of the plexus caught-captured
                    in a very good year of the sun
                double-decker   spotlight
It takes a million years
     for a photon to go
          from the sun's center to its surface
My journey is now the secondary "zip" it finds
                    that is its freedom in space

The same velocity your kiss imparts
     when all had been such secrecy
          he who keeps the secrets has forgotten

An escape so all-inclusive
     nothingness is then preferred
     a flight to blank beauty either side the road

A coppery arrangement of rows
I am fluttery with adrenalin
    where line-of-sight is longest   right-angled
      with lesser   more occluded directions
        following mathematically
          gaps   at certain degrees

All of this seeming to pinwheel   west and east
    like the work of migrants   hurriedly reviewed

It's 12:30, make it p.m. if you like

Did I say that there was orange?   there was!
Then   in quickest succession
    a pet shop with cypress
    Northwest Sporting Goods
    Yocum's Body Shop
        a Shell

All in Willits, maybe
    but actual towns are strangely unrecognizable
Les Schwab won't tell
And the Edgewater Motel just wants your money
There at the edge of virtual woods
Oh!   sleepy-bye!
    the day deceives
      wants you back in bed
        like a student of the graveyard

There was once a man come out of retirement
A man   eager
    to play his piano for the Bicentennial
I don't think he practiced much
          or made it all the way out
But if it's Willits I drive at forty miles-an-hour
    this is where his recital should have sounded

An ambitious program
    the LIST of works
      might have been all the program ever was
The pianist?   Al
It was a long time ago

His projected "Willits Romp" was a concept
                    performance art as inclination only

Like the mostly yellow Shell sliding by

This may have been the way the Gang of Eight went
When it went
          somewhere veering seaward
                         on a dangerous road
They were friends aware of China
          those fall-guys in Beijing
          the Cultural Revolution

We'd be twice those villains   fresh as daisies
And present our poems
      as eight
         as groups of three
            of five
               the combinations possible
Though barely relevant   as far as world politics
We were dear to ourselves
                   and that did certainly suffice

All of this dying to happen in Willits again   right now!
There's just no personnel to make it happen
The stand-in establishments try
                    but their auditions are off
Al   and ALL our bodies   beyond repair
And close the shops if repair was ever
                    what you had in mind

I've brought no pets   what if *they* died?
By the way   "yocum, you do vocals?
            you sound kind of country, you know?"
Hey! those Goods got the goods!
There's a Sporting chance
      the Northwest won't make me too sad
                             to see Harry
             I'm endangered as it is   without you!

Laytonville   being close to it
Being moved to let the video roll

12

that will replace the brain
we'll see if it can

The road is repaired   rebuilt   east side the valley
A bus would be better
A bus was always better   before
    when we'd take it
        staring   with no responsibility
                to stay on the road

The calendar's dates fluttering down
                like carefree autumn
Comics in my lap
    for when I tired of the window's movie
    or darkness left it flapping in the projector
        and landscapes went undercover

Now   in Laytonville
    without a greyhound
    without a ticket
        the gas tank empties accordingly
And a glance is the briefest of movie trailers

It's witness protection   a new identity
It's Laytonville
    where I'll learn the language
              well   its accents, anyway

Geographic separation
A good ear will hear it
    a vowel's very slight variation
    the rate of staccato that speeds the consonants
        a region's refinement of the standard
The changes so gradual   going places
    it's like the transition from the sempervirens
              to the Douglas Fir

Or ranging much further   to Arabia

Let the cell phone capture what it might
Fish-eyed
    the improbable screen   selective

                                                wanting to help

I'll blend in
See if I'm right
        in choosing the town with the blue mountains
            that are slightly that color   nothing being overdone
    See if I'm right about that, too

Near to the Laytonville Gas Company,
        Harwood Road leads to hideout's acres
The Chief Smokehouse   and Laundromat
                                    will become familiar

No revenge will find me
Or if it does
        I'll be putting bleach
                    in the little trapdoor's chamber
            and too much detergent just to make sure
                and downing something smoky
                        while I'm being smoked

Oh, and that third lane's arrows?
It is a middle lane that perplexes
                    being too suggestive
I'd drive in a circle if I paid too close attention
yes!   the fat white directions
                            left
                                oncoming
                    which way did the bad guy go?
                    and what on earth
            was my testimony?

Snitch?
Would I have done that?
The trial was long and windowless
I'd have to date the court recorder to remember

The rattlesnakes there are have gathered
        for a summit just shy of eighteen hundred feet

There's no warning
You're over it like the last bad dream

                         before the Lottery paid
Chance reptiles crawling
      in an afternoon made a mansion of contrasts

The eyes' dilation needs unbroken shade
There's almost a rhythm to the sun's exceptions   flitting

Hold the snakes to account
       and tell the young ones to go easy on the venom
There's the right amount
           and then there's youthful overkill
Is there parental oversight in snake world?
Or does guidance have no meaning?

I grabbed a few
The bites gave answers
       the bites as varied
            as wisdom's sayings may be
                and not kill the seekers of truth

And those same seekers stay   sometimes
En route to the truth   in abandonment
In a roadside graffitied
       some squatter-punk palace
       "CV" painted large

The cement receives the initials   and others
The "underground" above ground and proud of it

Shell of Grunge
     the concert
          the posture some nights
When Portland and Seattle got to be too much
And the kids hit the road
       the Ninety-Nine Percent dispersed   diaspora

I'm plastered   just thinking
The party about to break out in broad daylight
                   the proffered joint appearing

There's a cyclone   but just the fence of it
Enclosing windy protest

        that starts with freedom and goes elsewhere
           hollow as the compound's ersatz command
              the center not holding for very long
                                        at all
The windows' dark eyes saying admission is free
All in the green container and corridor of Nature

What mile marker is it?
The number a shared knowledge
                of refuge on 101 of course
"Just down the hill from Rattlesnake Summit
Find the safehouse   find truth"

When the road is finally four roads   the lanes
                                  parallel

Remember the hole that was made for a river
    the engineers disdaining to go much around
      preferring to dynamite
           and have a tunnel for the water
                     albeit   barely an arch
                     the mountain
                          cold-shouldered

We saw it once
The Indian closeup
     accomplished down-slope   and exploring
     a miracle cure of Outdoors

Whose friend you were at the time
Well, it may only be narrowed down
        like the river   its confines confusing

Yet the recon was a good one
The location an affordable dream

Some diary explains it better
        or   what was explained
             went on to become a book
                    of dreamscapes

And now   somewhere in these curves   in the place
Will you find it for me, love?

We'll down-climb too
    and see the river pour
        brand new as the rock!

And still together praise distance later on
When the only vista steals the show
    and lets us see to the south
        what was altogether shaded and occluded

All those forests
    and their bears
        expressed as wrap-around
        flat screen
The dimensions squished by faraway
    when treetops are a graph

Harry, could you join us for a moment
    and allow us to hear your interpretation?
Ask if metaphor applies?
Or shall we just call it scenery and be done?

I think Brahms coincided
He may be enough of an explanation
    beauty and indifference taking turns at the wheel
Brahms's Second Serenade it was
Second and counting

And what makes it a serenade and not a symphony
    is a thought the sound destroys
    and that is exactly as it should be
The music like pleasant parents
Those who prefer
    to just occasionally babysit their children
        trusting to a governess the rest of the time

There is a lowering of the highway
So gradual you refuse to call the asphalt unlevel
    refuse to pronounce the road an incline
But everything the river does   the road does
        in tandem

It is simply down   ever so gently

In the cold that is November
    the hard part is remaining stable
        keeping that part of the brain engaged
            that usurps regrets
The Peg House ahead is the best bet
Go on in there, why don't you?
    and peruse the trinkets
        what twenty dollars can or cannot buy

There are choppers in the parking lot
Their motorcycle madness barely held in check
The machines are unattended
They are pretend-hogs
    Marlon Brando being tired
        and far from Hollister
And the hip-talk is slower   without fan urgency

Note the fake patrol car
    positioned to warn
        and be mistaken for police
It is crammed with dummies
    who will undergo no crash test
            and stay seated
            as plausible fuzz

The words "South Park"
    pronounce a sense of disassembly
    of objects strewn
The shell of a school bus atop high-clearance
      assuring the child of wilderness
        is brought to the classroom after all
A Grand Opening perhaps
"South Park" a teevee meadow
    waiting on censorship's instructions

There's an ice chest belonging to leprechauns
    who keep their emeralds inside and cold
        their version of treasure
            green stones for the green-minded

Can you listen to your voice uncritically
Does it try to tell lies?

Can you hear this better than anyone?

Brahms   his Serenade once more
There are no words to it   no one'll fib
The Ninteenth Century saved
    as if the origin of all true affection were heard
        and the word "kill" left out of the score

To the extent no blame will fall upon the parents
    to that same measure   will fortune be found

The text of even the forest did not sound genuine
You wanted assurances its heart strings were tuned
    before its own serenade

There's a book deal could require it's clear-cut
Everything is Love   though it might be made of stumps
    the eyes and ears   sensitive to meaning

Those combinations
    of yellow and green
        in the central region of visible light
Every nuance
        when the forest is background   peripheral
        and subtly transmits saving
                and doing

Can you listen to your own poetry?
Or will you find it dead as remembered affection?

Sixty miles from the Crescent town
    music is imagined
        that makes of post-mortems
                a witness to rebirth
There is a pause
That   not-wanting-the-cessation-of-looking ahead
            being happy in advance
            Harry still awhile to go

And although it is a very familiar adrenalin
    with no performance involved
    unless good manners are that

there's a "backstage" to it all the same
        and the prospect of tardiness

Harry, I'll be there!
But the speed limit laws   well
    they can't be broken
        I have too many points
            went too fast too often!

Speed reduced anyway
    to be in Rio Dell and Scotia
        two towns   one Chamber
           where the Commerce starts
                the Chamber a gallery

A museum beflagged like the moons of near Space
Far as we can go
    for it's so very hard to go much further

The new median's a helpful divide
The barely employed were successful   what next?
Pacific Lumber was Life itself
Or Super Life, perhaps!
    more than nature intended
        in taking thousands of years
                    to make any changes

The lady's dressed in black who greets
A formal sort of melancholy

"Time was   time was"   she seemed to say
The narrative brief as closing time
    the outside sign retrieved
        and the one-storey village
                is a village entirely shaded
Unhurriedly sad   as last light in the second-growth
    whose hills have made the pavement blue
                    artsy, even

Highway 36 is the next question   asked eastward
Have you been that way to the Sacramento Valley?
And do you remember

    the way the road seemed aimless
        once you ran out of lowland
        and went high   hiding in plain sight?
Road that was an up-and-down story
      whose chapters were homesteads
        remote   and uneven?

And at first you were told it would take half-a-day
But the mileage makes the driver a skeptic

"Naw!   two hours, tops!   I used to race!"

36 is the Wild West with no power to fly
Alton   its true commencement
The bluffs surveyed   and white buildings
Like beginning thought
     that goes on to say wonderful things
     that are barely whispers
        and barely suffice for "Eclogue"
        Cesar Franck's single-digit opus
                     preparing to accompany

And you're not going to get anyone better
Better than Cesar   the Belgian
     letting E Flat Major fully sound its pastorale

The late afternoon has plans
Though a work-stoppage is also planned

Late afternoon   we'll see the guests
The guests from Motel 8 in Fortuna
See them off to work   and work through supper
Go without
     as they board Peterson's caterpillars
     and break out of the lot

I see them riding all over
Getting pushy and bulldozing
     just to see how much damage they might do
                           by sunrise

And what if no one minded?

Watched it like a show?
Made it a dusk-to-dawn-and-beyond picnic?
Their minds adjustable   accepting   attuned?

Four questions
    concerning beautiful flexibility
                                      perhaps achieved
    yet as unlikely as a world saved from itself

Watch the rampaging yellow!
Aloof   detached
Watch and not mind
And   magically, then   ironically   triumph!
                                              Fortunate!

We are now at one with the Wyott tribe
    who at Fields Landing welcomed Fields ashore
      his apologies accepted
        what did he do, though?
        unknown   never you mind
            it's not even known if he landed

Dennis Miller's talking about America
He is finding it hard to stay within its borders
It's another screed all right
    his description of Nancy Pelosi is worth it
    he took a right turn after Hollywood
        but it does takes two wings for a bird to fly

I'll listen to him a little longer
      who said that?   "two wings?"

Where'd that sun go?
Was there acceleration?
    faster spinning done?
      the planet in a hurry?

A spell of the Wyott, perhaps
Their shaman aroused
    to make a point before resuming his ritual
    the ceremony to include a brand-new myth

Power of the clouds!   cold and wet
Setting the sun more quickly   trapdoor grey!
I am following the lines
    as if this were an extremely spiritual affair
    set in motion by an undisputed master

I'll stand out from the rest!

No, wait!
That can't be right   the teacher would never approve!

Via Appia
Though the trees are wrong
    they're spaced like Italy
        either side the Roman stones

It was an intermittent fog
Just enough to have a second go at evening

It will start with Table Bluff
    this second twilight editing the day
                long distance
While a green encroachment borders Humboldt Bay
Close-in   dangerous, unsolid muck
No one trusting it
    but believing in its beauty
        its slime   its algae
           whatever Roman words it's made of

Say once more   giant lagoon!   "bay" is wrong
South Spit seeming so near, though
    you think the map to be untruthful

So brief is that green
    a coast side is made ephemeral
        witness protection's sudden failure to protect
        and soon enough is betrayal found
Strange sacrifice
With a moon still waxing   ready for more.

In Eureka   Carl's Junior's an observatory
So much observed in so short a time!

and at an optimal level of expertise!

Its scientists are patron astronomers
Wanting calories all the time
    their appetites for space linked to a menu
                  and dependent upon it
The more they discover   the more they order
The photographic plates put to good use

And there's that moon getting bigger
Getting higher up, too
    and getting bright ideas of its own!
              a backlog of them
Could be a new crater will be made tonight!

The entire city is learned   forefront
The average IQ nearly two hundred
And that is why   so many times a day and night
   is heard, "EUREKA!"
     bass-baritone   tenor   alto   soprano
                            sopranino!
"EUREKA!"   ideas with extended warranties

Other words than what you thought
And Carl is pleased to play a part

I need a cat like the one in Orick
A mother set in motion by her motel's guests
A warm robot triggered by new arrivals

The Palm Motel was her home
And after the manager   the signature
                      the key given
After greetings exchanged with neighbors
    just hanging   camped on their doorsteps
        everything dimly seen   in the late night
            three friendly syllables only between us
Mother had appeared
   a wide-awake fussy-bye

She'd been accompanied by four ghostly children
    playing very hard-to-get on the Velcro porch

    where slats hid the windows
        and red doors opened and closed
                in the off-season
Main Cat and sub-cats   a loose association

"All I have is Life cereal to give..."

What would happen?
Perhaps the Orick Cat would eschew?

I'd closed my door for awhile
    at home in the bed   I'd wait and see
      while someone was busted elsewhere
The interval of our knowing just a little patience

Two hours   then I opened
She'd been there   right outside   a valuable alien
    rolling   even as her kittens scattered under

"Let me give you Life, my pretty!"
    remembering the Witch (there's only one!)

I did give it   and her bites
    turned to crumbs the biscuits dispersed

There'd been a pool like a greenhouse   emptied
My nearest neighbor told a story I could not follow
        being cat myself from the contact high

Again I spoke to Egypt
"Hello, my darling!   do accept the grain, the wheat!"

The little ones were sheltering
The KIA was there   and they were under   well under

"How can I say, 'Goodnight' to you, Orick Cat?
'Good day' then   and when do you sleep?
Are you waiting for the sun like the Beatles?"

I was sprawled like herself by then
A feline spell   indiscriminate   I'd happened by
The red door wide open

I had had no accidents
It was the will of the Orick Cat
    I should survive to make her acquaintance

Next day   the white car is causing meropia
Palm Motel itself is a bright pavilion squared
No political consultants wander   no news is heard
There is just a cook's trailer and finitude
    the prospect of breakfast   magnificent
        as knighthood conferred on ne'er-do-wells!

Lime is the morning color
But other greens embellish
    and support the enterprise of motel
There are green poles sturdy   in all that vacancy

The pool needs water
The plants by the pool need water
They live
    or maybe they don't
        in pots like crowns made
           they are outsized adornments
                tidily arranged

There's every manner of planter
Someone's a gardener unafraid of side-effects
The azaleas are lovely
    like a long-sought reconciliation
      or invitation   to deviation

A hundred years from now
    a shinleaf will be taken
    to commemorate the place
        if it is still around   or even if it isn't
Plays enacted in the performance space of parking
Two stories   two versions   of Orick Cat
The world's and my own
    while guests and would-be guests applaud
      from porches and balconies everywhere

There's a dog at the cinema
He just lies there   a creature left over

left over
like the Orick movie house
                    with the blank marquee

The waitress said
    the last time there'd been a show
        she was still in high school

Today's delicate shadows flit
                    and windily decorate
Their tracery's the only motion picture now

A ghost girl's bicycle is parked
White   like so much else this morning
She's first in line at the Orick Theater
    waiting for Jimmy Dean's last movie to start

Alaska's on the wall at the Palm Cafe'
Some flag of the north!
Is that a Dipper?
Do I see Polaris in the weave?

Don't go until the staff is questioned
    and the other flags' other states found out
But there's no certainty to the interior
For the coffee trembles
            with unexplained reverberation

There's something British there!
That Union Jack!
Enjoy the room
    the cook staring straight ahead between orders
        pictures coming to life
        like framed YouTube videos

Pay   while the waitress is near and convenient
The counter just the right height
    and the menu a medium-length poem
                with plenty of imagery
Evolution's made it   and I must read it
Noting dishes gone extinct
    or so hard to prepare   no one ever orders them

Redwood Creek has knowledge of tsunamis
But let's call them "tidal waves"
               now that "tsunami" is general usage
Return to the misnomer   just to be corrected
The trench out there is preparing a Big One
That we know
        Cascadia must slump!

It'll be big news on a day like this one
A dog asleep on the sundialled sidewalk
               gritty gray   and warm, too
Fishing from the bridge in progress
Guests checking in-and-out of the Palm Motel
The sea will be sloshing forward and back
     as if it struggled with a grave indecision
     making all the difference it can
                   amidst aftershocks

All the stools in the world of counter cafés
        will not be enough hominess then

Terwer Valley
A green sign says so
It has a highway   the 169th
I don't belong
     always wanting things handed
        always wanting belief in pretending

The reality is Terwer
They worked for it
     the junction's gas adjoining small business

It's country   and what do you do as stranger?
Admire the gables, that's all
     do not interfere with Terwer's pursuits
              do not come calling, even!
Consider it sample turf with specimens left alone
Research here will lack conclusion

Turn anyway to follow   without appraisal
this route going home

                    to houses built for getting lost
Turn   mouth-breathing past bucolic fields
An American cartoon at large in otherwise lands

Fall in line like the soldiers did
        who went a long way off
            so very far away to settle an issue
                keep Terwer secluded
                the valley unfound by Axis powers

The dashboard bears have said the scene is default
They eagerly observe everything with furry premonitions
They go without sleep
            without supper and brunch
It is the kind of concentration
            only the inanimate are capable of

Their attention spans are spending plans
Profligate   unlimited
A great fortune
        that infuses the driver
            on the Klamath road   the river glazy
                            a widespread bed

Beyond the signage settle down
Dare to prolong the side trip
                    in spite of a schedule
For the idea was always to pretend
Pretend one is eternal enough
        to know the whole coast
            in such a way
            individual histories
                all its inhabitants are learned
The exact number of deer   of squirrels

Singing, "Let It Be!"
Questioning only those "words of wisdom"
And whether Mother Mary's in any condition to travel

Oh!   the many suns of the Klamath!
Their multiple beams
            a collective glitter

>   to go with a concept of immensity gathered

It's a high-rise highway as well
        that's left and right   around the bluffs

Drive on
Through oscillation's payday and dalliance
As if the forest were juvenal
        a plumage in tandem with the birds that shelter

Turns out there's a Terwer Creek
It's just water
Call it a creek, though
        and "Klamath", yeah   it can be a river
            when we're talking
The terms wearing down
        the way creeks and rivers do

That's social usage alone
There'll be another dictionary
        and   only "inhale/exhale" written now

Hey!
That Columbia's a trickle
And the spring-fed start's
        a raging consequence of an ice-dam's collapse
            somewhere Missoulan

Cross over! Cross over!   Terwer Creek
A waterway's mess of boulders
Their perfect asymmetry a greeting
        and getting wet   little-by-little

Arrive Oribelli's
A good place to eat and drink
                        dance if you want
And entering   there are three
Just a little conversation going on

They're a trio of voices
Barest patronage   more a social call
A couple of the boys

        to see the barmaid
Once inside   be a part of it   a stranger's part

No music playing
So the words are clear in the acoustics
Nothing shouted
      the place built for many more of us
It's a lull in operations

A man is offering his house and his boat
        to me   the stranger
        he says to go down a certain road

"Here's the address
      if you want to settle, mister   now's your chance!
      be happy to show you around
                      uh, where ya from?"

I said where I was from
But I was thinking   Terwer Valley

Oribelli's was vast
An emptied place   powered down
The woman behind the bar was kind
There was rhythm in our talk
      the pickups parked might never leave
          if they did   Oribelli's could close
          if we all left it's final

The woman had said
      to find the river past the dead-end   and I did
where the gravel became a gravel pit and turnaround
I'd be right back the way I came
But the imaginary fishing first!

And thinking of those cows beneath the trees back there
                        highway 169 come to a stop

There'd been cars to go with the herd
Bunched machines
           maybe derelict   in yards and lots
Cars that couldn't run but stayed in place

For there was not a good enough reason
                              to be rid of them

Is this a place we knew?
There's a berm   something raised
     a railroad abandoned, maybe   trackless
A levee so the river doesn't claim the town

It floods   they're safe on Shakespeare Street   intact

It's the season the trees divide
Deciduous and evergreen separate their limbs
                         the barren   the adorned
Here, the park has a city and not the other way
Its vast clearing
     like a green airport planted with old growth
A glade with a mayor
     whose bespectacled sight
          was still good enough to make a plan

Go back
And be satisfied Anywhere has its majesty

Don't worry!
The words "CHO TOK SEE MEM" are saying it
At a turnout   with light blue underlining
     and the phrase
     in brackets' red wedges
          either side
          like a tribe still in control
                         and mythologizing

There's a chief in a truck
Also light blue   with a white streak the length
     driver's side door ajar in a cafe's lot

He is there to admire the nearby emus
And wonders
     if Australia will be supplying other birds
          aloof as these   flightless
          parading away from close inspection

Paul Bunyan and his ox notwithstanding
It is possible to gain Wilson Creek
    Without interference
View the "Big-Granite-Rock-That-Broke"
                    (say it fast and more than once)

The Mystery is not the Trees
    but the concept of tourists
If they would only stick around
    the term would lose its charge.
They might come to prefer the little creek
And "Big-Granite-Rock-That-Broke"

Make way one more time!
I am thinking
    that Extravaganza's a beach
    a boulder field so crowded
        no passage is found   except around

There's no direction now
And every surface entices
It is arrival, surely
    a better plan
    than testing society for acceptance

The stone is unconditional
Says it loves me back
    before any declaration of my own

Is the wall unclimbable?
Even the best would hang in their harnesses
    rock climbing uncertainly   a 5.15z challenge
The handholds fantastical   climbing unaided
Too turned-over is the wall
    and gravity commands it stay unascended

But scramble, why don't you, what's possible
The wind is what to lean on
    back into   an air chair
And from that certain height above
    that is the seaward half
        of the Big-Granite-Rock-That-Broke

        be amazed that another beckoned
        the same as this one

Yet it is sufficiently far
    it merits a separate expedition
Wonderful   that there's more than one example!
It's almost open-mouthed
    a giant oyster pried   cathected

And where the second Rock-That-Broke is
There will also be a violinist   Sarah Chang
    her instrument cocooned against corrosion
    for the Sky God and Sea God do conspire
And her Strauss is rehearsed so magnificently!
Serenading the wind
    and ensuring I'll go there to be with her
        there at the second Rock!
To accompany!
To rendezvous!
    some day announced by the weather of concern

She can play all day long
Until the composer
    thrilled by the attention paid
        to all his musical directions
            signs on for reincarnation
            just to be within hearing
            and be a second suitor
                to whom I also desire

No matter if she's taken
Many husbands are possible for Sarah
    but only if she continues to practice

Of course she will
    for the world's disasters so need her bow!

Think promontory stone
Halved and weathered
Mostly an improbable copy of the first
    but graced with a musician
            a violinist!

Unlike myself   she's not a showoff
Rather   like the intervening waves that separate
     she has no choice in breaking
       it's what she believes
         because it happens
          in the blue day's solace
                and suspended history

And the solid rock that's broken here   has further cracked
It implies an hierarchy of fracture
              "v"- shaped   lenient

The seaair
     permitted to seek what it may in transit
In my mind   the parts are fitted back
Three dimensions at a time

Oh, heavy, heavy puzzle to solve!
     which   though its pieces are reciprocal
     like the coasts of Wegener's Atlantic
        they never budge back to their beginnings

Stone mirrors   massive with correspondence
Every facet refined

And sunward   above   in the minimal soil
     botany strains to say something, too
     swaying   but inches only
        with scrub's confinement   still
           with fundamental difference

Oh, glorious star!
     that makes the Earth's declension known
       and brings its light into interiors!

Then appreciate the log over
A log balanced
     like the grey bridge at Wilson Creek
               more than mere drift

It is timber

      the wayward post of a Samamish longhouse
Laid down and wanting totems
And where it rests till winter comes
      the log will stay a bulky still life
A henge   when the lintel is haphazard placement

Wooden connector
No circle made
Just the start of one   like this journey
      one that includes the city named for a crescent
The crescent found to be all-inclusive

Come with a warning label also
It's a tsunami zone all right
A vast   comprehensive hazard

So much for a tsunami to cover!
And   once-upon-a-moonlit-time   one did
              covering over and over again
              as is a tidal wave's wont

Nineteen Sixty-Four
It was Alaska's giant ripple spread
When the bottom dropped out of the trench up there

But today   business is sound
The sea is flat
      and nothing but commerce washes over
Proof no one's afraid

Signs do celebrate the dangers
They obliquely allude to sometime's floods
Though there is no hint of this
            in the Harvest Café
              in the Robin's Nest

A museum there is
Devoted to the telling
And there is more than one motel
                with water on the brain

It doesn't take much to make the ocean slosh around

And this bay's configuration?
    hell!   a jolt is all that's needed!
    somewhere   Japan   Chile

"I'm ready", says the beach
The same words my sister uses
    when it's time
        for the Oregon Ducks to play football
        or   her beloved Seahawks

Ready for the harbor to drain as it did before
And then   run up and run inland
In the lunar day
    and sometime night
        as clear as needed to evince

Supraluminal!
The wave train travelling
    and split by the lighthouse island
The worried tenders were a married couple
Sure the water would separate the two of them

And it almost did
Splashing and frothing in a false dawn's shuffle
We were told they survived
    when the easiest thing in the world was to drown
    for all   all   was oncoming!

The problem fell away   endlessly imagined
There   just before a bridge with the dunes
    named Tolowa   so far unknown

Dunes stabilized
So that one may count on them being there
    when you're good-and-ready to study their grains

I can hear the sands' rustling
And imagine
    how the rain must make them damply scenic
In a haze of Arabian thought   clean dirt drifting
A little at a time
        day-for-night   dimly enjoyed

The camera panning for all it's worth
Hoping to complete the movie
But the director's joined the cast
                        abandoned the plot

Maybe it was the acreage
The location undermining purpose
The dunes creating too many possibilities
                        for one film's dialogue

Struck dumb therefore   and speechless
We are lolling in Tolowa
      near to the river
      resting   in place of screenplays

Very undone
Like the incomplete trees
      that stump the pasture
           right side the highway

They are long ago gone to gray tables
In support of planters
        evolved to take advantage of the saw
           and fill in the stump
               with a topknot's foliage
Varied as all of ground-cover's possibilities

And   as if some knew it was aesthetic
                        most pleasing
The stumps were left undisturbed
Their several arrangements a notable affection

Before 197 asserts
      and its ribbon displaces
        what it needs to head east
Cross the concrete

Be in remembrance of pretty branches
And Tolowa's expanse that sinks production
      while it keeps to a shooting schedule
Gone past fame to what comes after

"Travelling without moving..."
      Frank Herbert! It's possible!

Ritardando and fermata
Milligal and milliluces
  the increments delightful!

Just shy of Oregon
  note the solitary evergreen
      that totalizes
Tree that's shindig and waving

Lake Earl's here somewhere
That prison, too
Pelican Bay more a theoretical body
  opposed to being found out

There's decline seaward
A very shallow angle, surely
A place where higher ground's a matter of inches
  not calling for "Gadzooks!"
      or any notice, really

Only green elicits

It would be time for a cheroot
    if tobacco were taught
But the road's likely to kill me sooner

It's official Oregon's the next state north
Think the border's a parallel?
Look closely at the quads that show the line
  and be shocked to see a series of lines
    making a slight accordion stretched
For the surveyors went point-to-point
     peak-to-peak approximate

Not a straight shot at all
Cross it anywhere and be untruthful

Two states are reference
Unsupervised conceptions

       still saying California and Oregon
                like dialectic materialists

Not a country   but a world   has fallen
Still the maps speak proper English
                and publish boundaries

To say it will soon be Oregon we come to...
To say anything   is certainly wishful
I'll drive on over the demarcation anyway
     experiencing state-to-state as an arcane joy
     wistful   as hours in the light
                  when they're really in the dark

What century it was God turned us in
                well, it's anybody's guess
But the captivity seems almost lenient
For Dread *only* presides
     satisfied a point has been made

There's no Last Chance
     though a liquor store proclaims it
        like a tax problem solved
        if you bought enough booze

Still six miles shy of ShipAshore
                in its grassy dry dock
The boat insists on resort status of some kind
Make a baby there
     you may put it through college
        before the infant catches on
Resort to other languages than human

The ship itself is fully loaded   with trinkets
It is a hull of narrow passageways
The merchandise irresistible in such confinement
     falling off the shelves into your shopping cart
There is the slightest of rocking motions felt
     though the last time it floated
     Washington swore his oath
                all six-plus feet of him

I'm seasick of the ship, I'm afraid
                    and it's pointed the wrong way
But it's still totable   needing turnaround

There is going to be rain
Like journalist tidings
        and tears   at end-of-time corruption
The highway masquerading as connection

All-Star Liquors, too?
Sure!   Why not?

Break their bottles!
Be the teetotaler
        hoping for stardom
                in a Temperance blockbuster!

Our ideas
        about what is male   what is female
        decided while we're at it   and not glossing over
The pasture encroaching

It is still America   perhaps more so than ever
And here at these margins
        Left and Right
            the coasts are in tandem
All may be well
Like dreams of the night and day entwined

Come to think of it   the sea is quite close, finally
The run to the border had been spacious so long
                it seemed a heartland's miles

And there's a hedge of full-grown firs
                    like a windbreak made

We were so far away across a plain   in coming
        the surf now is almost a surprise
                    absurd   so white!
        like the first time encountered
            a brand-new   energizing ocean!

The accelerator's hammer is further down than before
And a speed limit surely broken

Offshore   onshore

If you know when to look
    there'll be a seastack
        washed by waters seeking their lowest level

But there's one on the terrace, too
Haystack stone   its little island in the field
    proof the shore's unstable
        an elevator
           and sometimes down and drowning
Though its raising and lowering is an aeon's operation

And whether it's the sea or the land that lifts
        buttons still are pressed somewhere

Stick around
Stick to the subject
    the rock onshore's right there.   talk to it!

"What a child's mountain you'd make!"

When a grandma says, "sure you can go out and play!"
    I don't see why not
        but be taking grandpa with you, hear?
           he wants to climb that rock, too
                and not just watch!
Go ahead and see how far out to sea you can see!"

Ah! Brookings! Brookings!
I want all your boats to play with
    even the tugs   if there are any

There are very many masts
And mostly they bob   buoyant
    the white hulls hard on the eyes
        if you've just woken up in the Harbor Inn Motel
           and grope your way to the Pancake House

The second "ship ashore" rests
      but has not stolen the squat alliteration of the first
It is tubby
      and not rising to any occasion of commerce

Happy cops
      who make it here
          or grow up here
A small town where crime has yet to appear

And what goes wrong
      and who goes mad
          is moot enforcement sung
              to the happy tune of "Misdemeanor"
Your ~~cop coffee-and-donuts~~
      rarely   if ever   unfinished

Everything's riparian   "pertaining to a river's banks"
Banks themselves
      and the money inside
              a fluttery green

Strange dollars, too!
That must be spent inside the city limits
              and vanish if taken elsewhere

And it's an open city
Any army will do
Been declared open from the start
The azaleas thrive
      and Loeb State Park
          advertises the way to its delights

Flowers!
"The climate", it was said
      so mild there is never a complaint
It was also said
      to be an experiment conducted by the sun
And as soon as enough data's collected
              the town of Brookings would revert
To what, exactly   no one could say

Here, the traffic lights are long   on purpose
Are timed to detain and make you settle
                              all destinations forgotten

Okay!
That's reasonable   I'm easy
In fact   the port itself should really be seen
And perhaps the Coast Guard will explain its mission
And whoever's in charge
        will sing that Coast Guard song
        the one that's right up there
            with "Off We Go"
                and "From the Halls"

There are hoboes about
        with dogs and bicycles
        and asking curious questions
            just before the bridge over the Chetco River

Imagine giving them a lift
And then they don't stop talking
                        even for a minute
So duct tape   then take them anywhere they want
                        on your way

It would be all right
Certain travel requires silence
        except for cds
        and their inventory
            of Nineteenth Century romantic music

There's a hitch in the hiking
Thumb out   for a little attention   that's all
Give it and give up
Give it   and give them a ride   make room!
        the bicycle lashed
            and the dog in back

I don't know
It's not that much roulette, really
        and their vagabond hearts may steal your own
It wasn't always you had the means

Accept a gas donation   or don't

Staying on the road
     becomes more than staying to the right
         in some sense you're also left
            in stopping for them
Open to OCCUPY
     that latest incarnation of the Sixties

Could be a compromise
A lift for no politics
A ride that's hybrid
     and the generations mixed
            for thoughtful reflex

Experience the blend!
The everlovin' middle-of-the-road
State of Buddhist laughter and absurdity
     pedaled like a bike
           to out-of-the-way freedom!

Surprised by cheap gas
    I   and my imaginary companions   pay
    almost willingly
       the three dollars
          and fifteen cents of it   per
      in a Brookings station
           of colored plastic pints of fluid
The ATF   the weighty oil   so *not okay!*

And there's a scattering of orange cones
            demarking
               proscribing
Whatever cones can manage
     in their brief lifetimes   all hollow-pointed

Always wait
Do nothing
     for the Oregon gas crews
     they have the honor of doing it for you
You are monarch for a minute
Waited upon!

It's Oregon   it's like that   jobs   fall-back   default
Someone else will pump the gas

And it's gone to my head
I want more, now!
Want the attendant to arrange what's in the car
    give advice
    put me up for the night
    take dictation
    unlock the dream
        the mystery of why I come here
            to Brookings
            to all of up-and-down the coast!

Want him to spell it out
Type it into a template
But it's really time to go
    with Fred Myers peering intently
    and sober thoughts
        concerning Harris State Beach

It's just up the road
The place like a face   mazard   mask
    inscrutable
        assigning blame
            beyond easy understanding

Harris!
I know of one!
The first that springs to mind   yes!
    a war rembrance   in great detail

The Harris who bombed
    and theatrically   in Europe
    with airplanes visiting German cities daily
His thought was
    the carpet
    was all that was needed

"I'll prove it   and win the war   you'll see!"

But it's not fair to the park
    to invoke such a Harris
        such a face as his own
Rather the visage concerns as true a love
            as features can form

Photographically enlarged upon
Like first sight
    to a wedding attended by enemies only
      in the sense the presence of a crowd detracts
God will go away
      and the union falter

Love was always the reason
Creator of thoughts   and the words to express them
Love that's twins
    dual authors
      composing a draft to the Universe
        even the furthest Planet will hear of it
                ultima thule!

Help me!
I need to write!
I need to die!

Entering the park
With Mozart saving his best for last
His twenty-sixth piano concerto's slow movement
    is beautifully relevant

Well, it wasn't that Harris
The one who advocated all those bombs, oh no!

It was another
A pioneer honored with the naming
Had to be researched   had to be looked up

This is not the first time for Harris   for us
For time spent briefly
    following the route of old 101 to see it

Goat Island   close

Largest of the Oregon Islands
    yet too close to be an island, don't you think?

You're good to go to it
I'll wait   and prepare some sort of lunch

Oh!   you're an imaginary companion!
I forgot!   but all the better you explore it
Your reconnaissance
    will be all the more thorough
                  like an ideal

The writing so far will enter a slipcase
To await your report
    how many goats you found
        and if they minded your being there
Be goat yourself   with vertical eyes   and graze

I'm with you anyway
    to find whiskey in the layout
        that intoxicates what's found in earnest

All the offices of beachcombing undertake
With low tide's opportunities for employment
                as seaside jongleur

The day-for-night journey could end right here
For who should seek more than love?

Enter Harris
Enter into finale of language
The big island there has a name
    but it will not be used anymore

The trees of a scattered arboretum are still
Low pressure   and high   in balance for nativity
    for when the cradle is stable
        set down where the lawn is greenest
                on the manicured coast

We can't recall the baby's name
Being born so absolutely   it's better we're silent

It's right over there, that beautiful island
Mozart's island   with a piano   an orchestra
    Harris Beach hearing duple and triple time

Though everyone's in tune
    the Rondo has begun
        and there are no movements after that

Funny about that Eighteenth Century
It stayed away from this beach for so long
    it has to make up for it now
        reach its only conclusion
        before the rain resumes

Let the Japanese attend   and be companion beings
The rocks so need Nature back
    and a culture of observance
        the rakes to rake the sand
            between the basalt big art

I need the sculpture fixed by Alan Watts
Bridging the ocean
    to bring us zen the old-fashioned way
    before   you know   too many drugs

There's just enough stress
    to ensure the dampened rockscapes
                    are enlarged upon
Where magnification comes
            from the heart's preoccupations
The eye catching all facets
    figure-eighting the gallery's acres

No security was hired   the hours expanded
Harris is to be open 24/7 as long as love enters in
Even pictures   pictures with a flash
    permitted their lightning insights
        arrests   in salt air's custody

And knowledge is unexplainable wayside
                    and remembrance

Where the water has receded

and made those shallow mirrors
    a pre-storm sun is doubled
        tripled   and more

One is forced to reflect on   anxious to be relevant
   to human needs on special occasions
   when the soul may seek the celeste
      and play its heart out in proximity to stone

Samuel!   Samuel Boardman out of limbo
Details his largesse   and foresight
        in securing so much
Tells why it had to be done   the coast donated
How rescue is most pleasant
   his long   connected parts
       to include the Arch

His lengthy preserve elicits homage all seasons
In the gales   or quiet, exceptional summers
   pace to the memorial
    House Rock somewhere near
     to see inscribed
      the very short story of what he did

The parking
   though it severs the Coast Trail
    yet keeps it shaded enough
    for most of its Boardman miles

The lot is welcome open air
The artificial vantage forgivable   not stealing
No theft of the land
   or the rainbow that came to Rainbow Rock
    having divorced the peacock
    to be associated with condos
       crowding the headland

Lone Ranch   another issue
The creek belongs to its enterprise
   false promises gone to bed with exactitude

And after

After the milking   and other chores
      think you never needed "techno"
                        to find a rhythm
      running errands
            for the winds that make a prairie
                  of the Cape   Cape Ferrelo

Was it always treeless?
Perhaps it's the Ranch
      some computer in the landscape
                        smoothing soothing

"Make a good death
      and lie down for the duration of statehood"
                  pretending Oregon
                        outlasts geology
                        and joins the moon
                              in making rules

I said, "Believe and belong
      before Emptiness is judged a higher truth"
Haunting okay   in the sunlight, even!
As if it didn't matter   the condition of the clock
      with its one-way proposals

Get ahead of the night   and ghost the day
More accurately drifting   and translucent
So that no ordinary brambles spread
                        in the extant sitka
      but seem to burgeon by faith alone
      while the saplings add new inches
                        of lighter green
                        to turquoise
                        with
                  painstaking freshness

Like a godfather, Boardman explains
More than once in my case

And nothing adds up, strangely
The empty calendar flips
      stunningly irrelevant   with no free time

He sings a song last heard in the Fifties
When it was thought Heaven had relocated here
                              for the forseeable

Found Ranch!
Full of *objets-trouvaux*   from the extramarital
                                  from the cosmos!

I saw you exploring the creek again
      the wine bottle broken that held the vintage

The viewpoint built was personified
      and Samuel Boardman as well walked here
The Coast Trail worn
          with feats of agility and balance
The best acrobats have used it

In the afternoon's nearly level light
    the prospects
        north and south
           keep their secrets
Let's go and catch up with him
Revisiting eerie tunnels through the understory
    defending principles
      thought to be lost to poverty
        taking tough stands
          when to do demonizes your pet canary

The best place we could be was a catered lookout
Phantoms so happy you made it
    they arranged for sustenance ahead of time
                              manna
                              no charge

We are poor minorities
Caught a break and broke free of surgery
The City still looking for us   though in vain
    to reclaim its only children
        being jealous of humility

Stumble to the bench

For composure   for preliminary gratitude
It isn't every day that Oz abides the world
                       and greens it with   witchcraft

And though the Munchkins hide   as they did in '39
No doubt the day has reversed its beginning
                                       and end
With morning allowed   at last its own p.m.
And the rotund mayor of the Munchkin City
     consults his pocket watch
          impatient prescient
            for he knows Judy's house is due
                at Cape Ferrelo any time soon!

It's sandy down there
     outdoing Arabia one beach at a time
        in spite of the boulders' apprenticeship

What's uncovered is a six hour home
     tides allowance
        whose damp furniture's a comfort zone
Where you live   and set your fireworks off
As if Independence had strayed from the 4th of July
        and scheduled cherry bombs
                  for the rest of the year

The paths besides are toll-free   *non plus ultra*
You are welcome
     every which way on the bluff
Like thought   and near-thought
All the gifts of the ironic fog that rises
     suddenly authoritative
        like an Office of Nuance   now hiring

I cannot sleep just because the sun is out
Better to follow root systems braiding
     worn of optimism's miles
       the entire coast to walk
          and be tented   self-sufficient
No tripping   no hurry past the Sitka's architecture

Or let's not

And say we did
    the whole route   down and up
    too big a sonata and symphony
And besides
      Elsewhere
      would go unseen

No other life than this one
Let brevity and summary suffice

Or think
    a close encounter
      with the Cape   Cape Ferrelo
        this is enough to see the rest
As the blind may have better sight than the seeing
      Sometimes
        someone caring enough for that

The Christmas trees that bunch like delicate youths
    experimentally alive
    new to every proposition Nature makes
They are happy to frame the grass walkway green
In spite of usage
      beyond the posts spaced
        to stop a car bomb
          all ten of them gamely proscriptive
            and teething

The bridge at Lone Ranch Creek has been removed
    for the winter
What kind of bridge is it
      that may come and go like that   so easily?

It is magic!
The unseen gardener   trimming his park
    shaping the hedges
    effortless as air
And the places it goes we have never been
      seem to prepare for us
      and all our friends who come

You have never been

And your friends have never been
                so   awkwardly contented
Boots light on the roots   parallel or lateral

The unknown Ferrelo
     whose paths are crosswise and lengthwise
     so one may not miss a thing

This afternoon you are remembering, aren't you?
Childhood   just   earlier-in-the-day
                     and plenty of time to get it right

Believe and belong on the day-for-night coast
And especially here
     marvelling that no other headland will do
     for bringing the heartland
                           to the continent's edge

A century of this
     and Mozart must revive
         think his musical thoughts again
             and other resurrections happen
               spontaneous winter calling the shots

When the south is seen not too much later
     it's Harris again
     the Goat a giveaway
         the island at a distance
             corresponding with omission

The ocean-going kayak is untested
                        that would let us visit
So we are yearning for now
For goats and grass of *that* island
         south and north together

Relacing shoes in the jocund bluster
The ungentle breeze is nevertheless helpful
     and happily displaces whom would walk there
It's a prairie wind like in "Oklahoma"
     "where the waving wheat can sure smell sweet
         when the wind comes right behind the rain"

And it furrows and burrows into all-around
Saying "Yippee-yay!" just as the musical requires

Let there be no Judds around
    to be jealous and make trouble
And if there are
        let them *not* be played by Rod Steiger
          for that Judd could easily have had his way
            and made the rest of the cast homeless
            partisans of lost causes
                    and happy endings

I took the direction best suited to see land's end
And tear apart the logic
    that says,
        "Don't jump! you wouldn't die!
        you're not tough enough
          for Saipan
          for no surrender
            that kind of control!"

The Americans had tried to stop it   the suicides
But the battle for life was a poor second campaign
And so the Pacific received many
                broken and washed

I kept past signs that spelled their words correctly
Sparse poems to help you get your life back
                to a new normal
The English so correct
    so very familiar
        one's parents are somehow involved

"Go here! go there! do that!"

I don't exist
And the hallucination
    that is Cape Ferrelo
        well, it's God's own deception
He's said so   in a baritone   if not a bass voice
Why was I not surprised?

He was making repairs to the Cosmos
I didn't even try to get His attention
                         disembodied as He was

If He can do anything
He should bring back Ferrelo
      that he may see how He's honored
        by these picnic meadows' long-ago Spain
                still trying to discover itself

Walk on
Where the grass is tall you are doubly enfolded
      the atmosphere and land
          erring on the side of caution

Making sure the outdoors is actually cozy
Has a loop to it
And circles the drop-off
      where the full extent of the sunstar's reflection
      plays out   with blinding symmetry
              emblazoning   shore to horizon!

Nothing will change
And the sea's bright testimony
      tells a story of its choosing
           with brilliant annotation
Pillar like a great insight
        amidst the black ink spatter
              of ruined seastacks

A midnight sun in the temperate zone
Its crystals smashed yet still aglitter
      more so, even   for having shattered!

And   rounding the bluff   retreat
All that brilliance at your back   and following
Go through the field again
      to higher ground
Rereading the directions' bible of three or four words

   Mute   precise as much as sunward overwhelmed

    with random
        chaotic shards of itself

Cape Ferrelo's prairies are on and on
Foreshortened through trance
Trace pathways disappearing
    for everyone here who could be here
      and feeling brand-new in the blustery afternoon

Reserve has crept into our Dyonesian persuasions
Like a team effort of all the muses
          to put in place beginnings

The shadow of the sleepwalker is keeping pace
In the bluff's deep pockets of grass sequester
              as if intending to remain

Pretend the breeze a rascally presence
All sides of an argument together
And the trail is green-slicing the rest of tawny
    in retreat from drop-off
      spelling backwards the words of outdoors
        for the cities' minorities shelter
                    of fallen brick and steel
Most of all Time was a cape like this one
            tread lightly today as before
The metropolis arose to beget delusions

Is there a Speaker in the wind?
Who said that!?
Whose secrets told that make a further mystery?
And why does this seem to comfort not knowing?

This is returning as well
    the world having turned that much to magic

Came to Indian Sands and the Thomas bridge
The high bridge over high trees and a creek
Bridge that my friend James Cagney, Jr. knew
    the canyon steep
        inducing acrophobia's butterflies

When look-down came
        unnaturally though irresistibly
When being on top of things is necessarily scary
Too easy to be above it all in just driving over
The engineering a lot of hard work we never did
    so there's an element of privilege in play

A czarist view
    feeling shaky in spite of the scepter
We're birds that needed steel to stay aloft

And Indian sands   that generic assignation
The mapmaker's infallible pretense
If they are "Indian" sands no *more*
    no more *call it that*
    though the two words have a life of their own

Those words do persist
    like a Salvador Dali clock draped
They bring you there easily enough
The brain children of alien elders
    and too much to relearn
        to live any other way than after-the-fact

Love the word, "Indian"
Search out its usage
    remembering Indian Beach and Tillamook Head
    how the beach was staging
        and wrap-around indigenous
        seeing their canoes out there
            despite every aspect
                      of the near-shore sea

How it froths
    about the boulders barely seen
        or standing to be counted
        as masterpiece stone
            brought together from tribal dreams
Their familiar profiles become fixations!

Anthropomorphic
Having shapes with the power to possess

If "Indians" apply
    a place may be searched for Indian meanings

And a ritual assessment made   depart
    having promised the sands   Indian Sands
                                    long-distant love
Those sands explained as best you can   activist

The soul's cd's a continuous sound
Music the most charismatic art
Die of suicide should it ever be forbidden
    for its power alone may be trusted to heal!

A moisture system   the creeks   the coast entire
The belated storm upon it
A simpleton's in charge
    who will change plans to sail
        and has an infant's sense
                          of what's important
knows a child's glance at uncertain weather

It's expert watering   a shortfall of flooding
The family submarine dry in the downpour!

Meanwhile   Hooskaneden's crossed
Creek with catchy sobriquet
    that interviews the fish who find its passage
                                    inland

Hooskaneden!
The name with which we conjure
    and remember the northernmost of Boardman
    where the surf's aquarium sounds the loudest
where   in the proximity of giants
                Nature overrules the faint-hearted

Every monolith begging for composers' names
And receiving them at last   with supplications
        and the singing of entire symphonies

The hillsides are terraced such
    no elevation lacks a level place

      the woods there   kindly   supplemental

In the naming
    the Romantics won out over earlier formality
        though Mozart and Haydn made the final cut
        and all the rocks saved themselves for later
      in a classical way
      and conserved their stone
              accordingly

The wonder was no others came
Where, oh where are the living!?

It was as if the cove were off-limits   a secret
A counterintuitive terrain
    where music played as you passed each seastack
    all that was necessary?   pronounce the names
      the proper names of the composers
        for whom the sea stacks are named!

Something they wrote would begin.
Many melodies were possible
    the Bach Rock   the Haydn   and the Mozart
A tongue-in-cheek situation
Like the best efforts of newly-minted Hippies
    really listening for perhaps the first time.

"There's only one terror
        fondling the city's streets and alleys now
That someone with more money
    in the bank of emotion
      may buy us in the end
      though we were the ones
        who'd invented passion
          and patented it's aberrations..."

Who said that!?
Were they hearing Schumann at the time?
Mistaking Chopin's harmonies for common despair?
Already so busy with it nothing else mattered?

Well, this is the extent of the operation so far

Be everywhere the Coast can go
    its authority and concerns as well
      please   a good definition of the word "purview"

I dreamt I thoroughly plaigerized because I could
Because SCRABBLE must be part of it   that dictionary
I wanted it that way
    and thought so much of the book
       the use of any word therein was stealing

Wanted it that way south of Hooskaneden
On the hoary strand
    thinking of the July Monarchy in Paris
    and who had come to town
      to miss Poland
       and be a part of that remarkable circle
        musicians
        artists
        and writers, of course

Now the road curves away
    is too familiar engineering
      that wants you safely moved
        as if by shuttle
         to Sebastian, the Cape
            and Hunter Island

Both devoid of ballet
Except for certain nymphs of the basement stone
Spirits in the winter waves
    that erased the trees
      with their constant scour
        of the lowest   fissured inclines!

Nothing in the name of Art applies
For the dastardly ocean conceived a better plan
    one that was simply rough-housing chaos
        put in overwhelming play

Hunter is also a road saved for later
Not next time but soon
A second life

lyricizing past the present tense of song and sex

This amazing littoral!
Like land-and-sea scapes disposed to persuasions
    that are a Genesis all their own
        no one's hungry
          Beauty's nourishment taken

This would be a perfect place for a shave and haircut!
Here might massage be done   and manicures, too!
It's perfect for push-ups   knee-bends
Anything that makes you better
      being better done in the dark and in the light
                              of these miles

The lumpy dunes are hiding something
I *know* it!   lost keys and coins!

This is where belongings go
     to be free of ownership   not subject to usage
This is where your "things" are kept   covered forever
Bad habits broken only by removal
     and buried where the land is stable
                      anchored by grasses

We are glad to find a natural setting
     not subject to anguish and carelessness

The pistols are placed to rust as well
Where their namesake river mouths the word for exit
     turns right and pools here and there
      still fresh   before once more finding the sea salt
Even the pistols that had no use

And overseeing it all is a single house   high
Higher than the cliff
    safe from erosion
        a neutral gray
           having no opinion
              the house being full of found objects

 Ah!   there's the large pool next to a land stack

It's rather halfway-in and halfway-out of the Pacific
    a rock that's hard to summit
        for it joins with the continent awkwardly
           just barely
                and climbing it takes you from land to sea
           as you stretch
                    for a fourth-class foothold

Oh, slippery basalt!
Would Mozart be doing this on his day off?
And if he wanted to make such a move
        would Constanza dissent?
           and say, "No, no! I want a whole man to hold
                        don't try it, Ducky Dearest!"

The pool has doubled the boulder's size with reflection
The Underworld will find it formidable
Just as unsafe
        there in the mirror
        surrounded by filiform blades

If the forecast holds   the pool should enlarge
The pointillist rain will dimple
        shatter its glass
             and begin a watery art school
                  staffed by mermaids beholden to no one
                          but Esther Williams

If you would know more
        about the pistol and its sequel stone
        stay and hear of that dark assemblage
                        photogenic

There's even an arch among the monoliths
Here it was
        the spirit world
        had some very serious business to attend to
The tribes were put on standby
        while the shamen tranced
            and tried to understand
                the story they'd received
                      from Indian mega-mind

Giants were involved!
There'd been a battle
All the giants were killed
    and only their weapons remain
        these gigantic rocks
        the arsenal left to remind

What strength it must have taken to heave them!
It's still not safe
    for the rage of the giants went into the stone
    and the very impressionable are apt to go mad!

Themselves walking at low tide
Around and between
    these unwary to then acquire
        the ancient animus
    resume the feud   perpetuate the struggle
Striving to push upon and move
    that which they cannot
    being merely human!

Further past the Pistol's mythologizing river
    the lesser river of Myers Creek has lent its name
Somehow   the drama's been entitled

Myers interpreting
Myers reporting

The course of his thought to include other explanations
    if you have the time
    the stories to start
        the way a creek gets underway
Almost imperceptably at first
In the nip-and-tuck gulleys of the high ground
    then swelling with narrative
        and a gravity-assist

There's nothing to fear if you follow his directions down
Down to the subliminal sea
    when you may act the part of monster
        with impunity

It is close to Christmas   but not close enough

The date?   sure
      November 15th, 2016
      the second day
The first was an interne's

A recent medical school graduate
      staying past a bedtime for tradition's sake
      all bleary-eyed in the operating room
A coast dissected wrongly
      while highly experienced
      gifted, even   associates
      just   stand   there   affecting no interest

We are in sight of the Yule
Close   but no cigar given to Santa
      the present of Gold Beach   unpresented

Hunter   that name   is back as predicted
This time a creek and not an island
It is difficult to say which may be proximal
      nearest a point of origin
      but if someone should insist
      "One or the other!"
      I'd probably go along

If the same Hunter's behind all this geography
                  we're bound to learn it

There's a ballerina who lives on a farm back there
She lets nothing detract from the barre
And she *pliés* to "moos" an "clucks"
      having *very* good concentration
      while her farmer-husband plays the piano
      carefully   for each exercize

She does not require a class in town
      preferring the creek
      to all that shouting   scolding
                  and counting

Much better!
They are very much in love
    and hunt for more of it in meadows and glades

All the ballet they really need
    is to be found in *Tales of Hoffmann*
    the Powell and Pressburger movie
For what is pictured there is paradox and release

Their dog is a pinscher   used to classical music
Even knows the keys involved
      and what it means to minuet
      guess it was osmosis

Their names are not germane
    well, okay   Gretchen and William   familial

And the reason for this mention is:
      their car is just ahead of this one
      any minute now they'll signal
            and we'll reunite

There's the gate to Gold Beach
From the south it's on the left
    cragging over   beaklike
    a chunk of Yosemite   but made of different stuff

Now both cars are stopped and we're catching up
Looking at the distant islands together
    losing the sun is remembering the moon
They want us to dine together

"Won't you join us for a night and day on the town?"

It wasn't possible
    being due so far north of the gold
      there'd be none left upon return

They excused
And   though it wasn't Christmas
    I gave them all the Mozart we had

and told them:

"Play it all!
    and think of our going
        as some sort of coming back   it's better!"

They said goodbye
The bird rock had said goodbye as well
    Gold Beach a very *temporary* entertainment

The Curry County fairgrounds are empty
Right over there in the emptiness   lovely to think on
    lovely the medals won
       the work done in such surroundings
But it will stay imagination's rodeo
                      if animals are a part
The last light's unable to illumine

The only fair that really mattered was Puyallup's
That one   so long ago
    first prize
    the other prizes   meant to commend
Prize hog and pumpkin
            Eastern Washington the judge

A day that father was on his best behavior
Did all the right things and didn't drive drunk
Curry County!
What's that?!
    a province?   Uttar Pradesh?
    a subcontinent's subdivision?

In Gold Beach   the outdoors is nicely boxed
There's certainly an element of luck
    where you find yourself enclosed
        with large teevees and other amenities

But do you really want more stuff?
A place to put it all?

the space of a car   make that enough
Gandhi left the world with just his sandals

Surely you can make do
    with what can be stuffed in a hybrid

The Cannery's piano still needs work
I'll spring for the technician
Since civilization has come to the coast
    we might as well have music
        live music
            keys that are properly regulated
                    tuned and voiced

It's such a delicate action
    play nothing later than 1800
    play nothing written after that year

More fake cop cars have been placed
There's no way to tell from a distance
The out-of-towner will slow to the posted speeds

Shelter here   and think yourself secure

As if there really is safety
Somewhere to be apart and excise oneself
And cancel   without suicide
    the sights of human progress

A hideaway   absurd!
As if there's an abandoned gold mine
    capable of making you a millionaire
                    of Brahman isolation
Hell!   the hectic planet will contest the delusion!

In the Visitor Center's center
    do not be jealous of a job
    that job with a view as well
The woman behind the counter has the job
She's the one   the lucky one   to be so employed!

And she's anticipating questions
Getting out maps
No "Center" so situated!   so scenic

Stopping by is doing it all   with medical benefits
A squeegee of the mind
    all is clear
    her summary superb
It is as if the ocean has a voice
The Rogue   a voice

The shuttered coast is personified
She's better than a wife
    no fights
    no explanations required
    no alimony payments

The whole place vibrates
Phases in and out of relevance
You just know what's going to happen

Have we made a movie yet?
Didn't think so   sign her!
    a fat contract for a very sharp lady

Create a role suited
One that does not even require
    that she leave her present position
    ambassadorial
    and already starring
        in a day-for-night walk-on

Let me channel Svengali
And convince her I'm right for her movie house
    the coming attractions not to be missed
    when we lay out maps and lay upon them
        crinkling
Something in the blind body's domain to make content

Visitation like a home invasion
    agreed upon by both parties
    in the Center of affection
Who will call it a crime?

Vote with Dyonesus   your heart's provisions made

Not to belabor any trust in so-called authorities
But two officers of the law
    Said that Astoria was seven hours   really?
And what did asking mean?

If hours were your measure
    then lost is your treasure
        that trove comprised of emotions

And they do damage
The clock's unwound that would tighten the soul

Time   the friend
    if it will end at last
    and be only a theory of forward and backward

I'd come upon sheriffs conferring
Their windows down   their driver's sides aligned
It was to interrupt I asked how far to Astoria
    to test their attention
    get a tax dollar's worth of it

Checked into their break
To see if good driving might result
No more running red lights
    and taking one-way streets the wrong way

Interaction   save a ticket   get their ideas
                      and get order

Back on the main drive
    and passing Gold Beach Inn and Pacific Reef
    "how long" *anything* was no longer a plan
Saw it as sickness and knew remission

And   assisted by lysergic acid
I stared at my fingers
    each one a different color
And wondered what music they should make
                  in such a condition

  Gold Beach was chilly

The last-minute sun
    yellowing the hills beyond McKay's Market
    where customers are shopping
        as if for the end of the world
        even the canned green beans are gone

Did we suffer an invasion?
Was there a Second Coming
        and a Third   and counting?

Get the book while you can
It will be a gift for Harry
Husband
    of the woman who was mother
            to whom I have loved so much

And though he is a widower
Because he is that
    there is a book I'll find
Some book he'd like
And so stay in love with her so very indirectly

It's right over there   I'm sure of it
Let's go   without depression
    to the bookstore's shelves
        the history section, of course

There, now!
There it is
    a thick one about the last millennium
Perfect!

Take it before the confusion of choices
It's not a chain   there's only one store
    and though the locals are prolific
      no question   *The Last Millennium* it is
        skip all other titles

No wrapping   the volume as is   he'll love it!

Cross the Rogue and its jet boats
If you call it a sunset   the saying is delay

Bandon fifty-three miles from the mouth
    and those aquaduct arches
      not that they're Roman
        but their little "leaps" stay historical
          bridging the wideness of the waters there

In the blue day's finale   get used to crossing over
The means   barely visible engineering

Rachmaninoff was needed
Something sadder than late afternoon
Music to make a bridge safe   and no cause for anxiety

Not that those arches would fail
 Oh, no!   it is the metaphor that's faulty
      that which weakens by example
            steel   what it takes

Let's use the word "rugged"   it shouldn't be hard
Rugged's out there if you look
      the next island
         North Jetty
            cattle in a white expanse

Once   single-minded   Gretchen and William came here
    and drove the road where all the houses are
      edge of the pasture
         built as far west as possible
         without falling off the edge of the continent

World-class construction
The investment to include indescribable beauty
They'd said it was a row of houses
The whole world was watching
      and hoping some were for sale
                             they weren't
Would be like toppling a government to get one

And though millions were offered
    the money was met with yawns
               and disapproval

You can't always get to this level
But such was the living and the dying
    enlightenment came easy
    every few minutes in fact
Mansions in tandem   synchronized
Interchangeable households
        the unruly universe jealous of the anomaly

Most amazing, perhaps
Everyone who lived there was drug-free
        not so much as an aspirin taken!

There   on the straight boulevard near to North Jetty
They'd shut down the shutdown
    promulgated by madness
    and switched on that which leaves well-enough
                            alone
The cows *most* grateful and unusually content
Having a sixth sense of the situation

Gretchen likened the experience
    to those days at the barre
        when all positions are suddenly effortless
Past practice   and knowing art
Like the solitary island out there
    that is reached by a determined gangrel
        for the purpose of vanishing at last!

We are waiting for rain with Rachmaninoff
Humbug Mountain a qualified bulge
    barely distinct from clouds' trafficking

If will begin   and the beginning's best
With those fat drops and general dampness
    it will be more dramatic
    for being a twilight's pouring
        into shadows' zones and graying out

There's a parallel road   like an after-thought
Someone making *sure* the traveler has a way to go

There's yellow "do not pass"

Dash-and-solid beginning to moisten
Still   the wipers are asleep
       like an underpaid projectionist

Look again
The Sisters more clearly outlined
    because they are nearer
    and backgrounding Humbug for now

Always angry or sad
    the landscapes and seascapes reciprocate
        all the hours day and night comprise
There is a rage for education
Studying while driving

Waiting for rain with Rachmaninoff
The oncoming headlights are lamps that pass you by
    and in such a symbolic manner
    you think you are missing something
               with every encounter
Double comets in retreat from an absent sun

Look!
An outlined cross   glowing
         apropos of nothing in particular
Pull over for salvation
    that oh-so-churchly word that crowds out secular

This darkness sells a liturgy
This graying out   a better summons imagined
    wafers and wine
    is there a Host?
Don't forget   even if you trust not a priest

Perhaps a service will find another way to impress
A *surprise* service   full of anomalies
As if religion got fresh and came on like a harlot

The next two-and-a-half miles   expect to see elk
A *sign* said that for two-and-a-half miles
               there'd be elk

Say "Ophir" on the same stretch
The park a mystery
    that does not weaken
        in the night of your music
Rather broadcasts those portions of itself
            that may be easy for you
          the accessible Koran

The center line is a double solid of concern
And it eerily divides the hidden herd

Near the end of the two-and-a-half miles
    there was a property   lanterned
       lumieres zigzagging the lawn
      all over the place   and pale

Starting the grade from Euchre Creek Road
The card game's a street
Or an avenue of Christendom reserved for pilgrims
            from a certain corner of strange

The dark woods darker than before
Whose inhabitants wear antlers and are unpredictable

Extra workers will be hired for the holidays
Where the lanterns are   soft-lit   sequential
    the children have left home
      their years illumined at intervals
A faint reconnaissance adding up to empty nest
With light to match the twilight

Rise to unstable slopes   and the Sisters group
How many?   make it a variable number, depending
Are they twins?   as many as a sextuplet's total?

Each is dangerous   the rock unique
Though barely class four
    there's oppression to it
     a black-gray that yields foreboding
Even the easy routes   one ascends uncertainly
           mindful of their charcoal hearts

The largest is carved hollow   sea to land
With branching tunnels
        so that the ocean pours out of and *into* its cave
                    the entire space resounding

Please no one explain the terraforming done
The purpose of the rock-strewn ramp from the jetty
I'm a kid   I get it before you've even started
        before you've said a word
            or harvested others' words from local history

The Sisters are my own   however many
However charged with enterprise

We saw the dinosaurs together
In the Prehistoric Garden we were life-sized as *they*
        thinking the Rex to be not-so-very Tyrannical
            now that he was actually encountered
                close-up

We'd been stingy tourists unwilling to pay
We only peeked at the brontosaurus
        and completed the stego guy
            with the clue of visible parts at a distance
"Better to leave something for later, anyway
There's only one BC garden in these parts   make it last..."

This   recited to Arizona State Beach
        deciding states make the best state parks
            starting with Arizona
Good name for a battleship, too
            if you're going to pick a fight

And oh, yes!
Be ready and forewarned
This prehistory   this Arizona just now
    is night's scenery
        and quite transformed is its use
Go from day-bright *then* to a shadowy *now*
Everyone vanished who took the monsters' measure

On approach to Port Orford

      the western sea's still lit
          just a horizontal piece of it
          Humbug interposing
          as if sales of sable were up

It was an avalanche of darkness
And where you stop to take its switchbacks
        was unknown staging
Those upper woods disappeared
             and only the creek comprehensible
           twisting   like the highway
              to one more exit
                that will be all-of-a-sudden

Like everything in the night

Sound is a summons
The summons full of chords the violin knows best

It's been a matter of months since I said I'd come
North to see him   Harry
He would be leaving for the east
     a much longer   heartbreaking journey
      away from the home he'd shared with Helen
                          his wife

Now   missing her   the west wouldn't do
It would have to be east he went
     and there were only days *until*

The Hybrid was important and mustn't break down
Pray it doesn't   think other thoughts than waking
      the sunstar finished
      that shone on Redfish Rocks
                  and the Sea Crest Motel

Think *danseur* and *danseuse*
Wraiths of evening
     outspending their allotment of phantasmal

Take their pictures the old-fashioned way
Pictures developed as soon as the shutter's eyes

for the camera-body records it all   are closed
    the road noise a soft accompaniment

And Sea Crest is outpost lodging
Worthy of a silent ovation
    was there vacancy, too?
        yes   a museum of rooms

If this were Italy
    one could say a *libeccio* had arisen
A southwest wind like a hardship
In the sense it blows in support of oblivion
    but not enough to complete the task
      so that one is only temporarily exempt
        from the Real World
That which we were told would be so wonderful

Let Port Orford be the finest small town
      where gale-force is permitted
        and not going to a doctor's a virtue
The winds given keys to the city
The Port can be that
    especially with that upscale gallery
    and bar as good as anything far south

The Bay of Bridges   San Francisco
Come to the country to be decompressed
"City" of one crane only
    that lifts boats one-at-a-time
    from the dock to splashdown

I'll enter the Bistro   Paula's Bistro   once again
Not locking the car
If they steal even here
    no point in publishing
Enter into After   the Afterlife, that is

But first see Paula   that's right
And renew acquaintanceship prior to carjack

It's just across the road

With the Shoreline Motel needing guests as well
    like the other place
    on a Friday barely 6pm

Here too the sisters went
Reconstruct *that* day that is now a night
        redly accessible   though unflashing
Wonderful to gain admittance!
For it seems a random establishment
                          open only sometimes

Paula's Bistro
    with dark cars parked
        and pale tables and chairs outside green-slatted
The burgundy exterior
        trying to keep you warm
           before you enter through yellow bricks
         double glass mistaken
           at first   for a doorway

It's a good thing I noticed
Though this guest had travelled far
    they have "reserved the right to refuse..."

First thing   and without asking
    I started photographing the art on the walls
Of course one is supposed to ask
But it was past bedtime
        and the wrong thing's the right

Started shooting
    the vase
        the paintings above the piano

Without thinking   I panned from one to the other
There was a marble bird
A peregrine falcon with mottled wings
At least I carefully avoided the pedestal
              that held it
                  precarious

Enjoyed the portrait of a woman,

     whose backward glance
         seemed a signal for rebellion

Examined an embrace portrayed.
As if the couple tangoed
    and this was the pause with the rose clenched

The painting of the girl with delicate fingers
    that enlaced her body
        a diaphanous white
           to offset those curls
               black as sudden misfortune

When confronted   it was too late to apologize
But there *was* an attempt and I *wa*s contrite
I tried to explain the brazenness
Paula's husband says
    "They're for sale   *all* of them   interested?"

He continues
    "It's all right   we have a connection
                   what can I do for you?"

"Clams!"

"Consider it done!   I will inform Paula!"

Still my mind was full of looting
And I couldn't take my eyes off the dalmation
    poised on a railing and wanting an owner

"Good evening to you, dog!"

There were books to read and bar bottles to count
The bar shiny   a long, drawn-out table
It transpired that no one was offended after all

The piano got some use
    a Nocturne of Chopin
It was now night
And I thought the mistakes made
    were like those pictures taken by a stranger

Just enjoy your favorite things
Half the time you don't mean it
      making oneself or anyone uneasy

I thought of San Francisco
It was a catnap made me ask
      if the City still loved me
      if the City *itself* had fallen from grace

When I awoke there were clams
Three or four were still frozen
      more mistakes   but I didn't let on
      the end of the year was near
A fresh start for everyone
A new digit   the number four

Like a speedometer   both three and four appear
A split at midnight
      that moment revolving
      2013 and 2014 dead drunk together

Will Port Orford's New Year find the Bistro open?
            closed?
                   or something between?

Paula embraced me
      grateful for the music
      as I was grateful for the clams

"I remember your sisters!"

And out there   not far
      the Port Orford Heads
          tried to make up their minds
          make sense of themselves
          of my visit
The walkways of the sea deserted
The all-weather concrete
            still in place and nicely connecting

On to Misty Meadows

      where the jam's homemade for Bandon
What keeps them holding on
          despite global warming

They wear the face Face Rock suggests
Though the profile's lost to Stygian night

Later crash in Hebo's early morning
Tired enough to call a parking lot a camp
The space beside the bar that *was*
            thoroughly vacated

Not even closing time
    and the weeds went on to explain
    that the liquor not only no longer flowed
      all its bottles were smashed
    by so many ghosts
        a ghostbuster would quit
      not even start

It had been easy to be unobvious
No one suspected for no one was up
Or at the most just passing through
    uninterested in vagrants
    especially those enclosed in cars

Harry, it turned out, had very shiny shoes
And we sat down for brunch and politics

He said he'd miss the dancing he'd been doing
Said he'd been to many parties
    musician friends
    and others keen on a proper send-off
        though none wished to see him gone

I was glad I'd come   and just in time
He was mentor, somehow
    my last chance for a father

The goodbyes I don't remember   by choice
Being goodbyes that were surely final
And so   to not remember some more

Harry's "son" drove Rainier Avenue
from Seattle to Renton
        that former Boeing town

Left the mighty beeline of the Interstate to do it
Knowing thoughts of 1951 would come
Year of another ride in that year's July
A family travelling
    train station to a new home
    having deserted the *east* to find the *west*

My real father greeted us and hailed a cab
And we went   Lake Washington on the left
    as it soon would be again   further on Rainier

Past the Vietnamese and Chinese zones
And the very imposing high school
    that once played us basketball
                   and probably more

Let it be nameless today

Harry had taken *me* out for brunch
Not the other way around like I'd wanted
    but *no* plan's been followed so far

This Rainier Avenue for instance
You just couldn't resist
    the long street to its namesake volcano
Well, *some* distance towards the mountain, anyway

Had no trouble finding it   the avenue
Four-laning itself due south
    just as reaching Harry's place was easy

What's *hard*
    is understanding how sixty-three years
        had turned against me and vanished

One moment   at the start of the first year
We'd been met at a train station

The next   there was a spaceship
              headed for Pluto and Charon
              the outermost
And Seattle was a spaceport with an alien skyline
One that made the Smith Tower a toy building
        once the tallest thing west of the Mississippi

Please, someone!
What happened and why?

Bette Davis does not understand

"Why do you want to see me this Sunday?
                      and so badly at that?"

But she will get it when she's told
We'll make it church when I tell her
        for I think she knows the answer to my question

Yes   it must be so   life is good
Rainier curves
        and vectors a little south-southeast   probably
Like that school, though
            you can't know everything in dreamtime

There's an Australian aboriginal driving
I have never been more behind the wheel
On the up-and-down coast   a native

Proceed   while the rain-sky sleeps off a dry drunk
      and pauses over Renton
        with a Martin Luther King, Jr. Way
            rear-viewing Berkeley in the mirror
              its own King seen
Connect the two and other links may be known

Are the tall trees either side relic branches?
Or have they only shaded since your exile?

The beautification's complete
All those trees and imminent rain
            did they really get that tall?

They look like a giant bower bird's nest
Without their leaves just now
        the Hybrid displaying

Down the middle past Genessee
    please be careful of all the bicycles!
With a wandering mind
    it would be so easy to collide
        and ruin everything
        be the object of eco-rage
        you and the rental stoned

Don't run reds, either
Not just now when getting nowhere
Doesn't matter
    wait until it does

Meanwhile
    playing red light/green light
    like the grunge tune,
        "Should I Stay or Should I Go?"
Be street-legal the length of Rainier Avenue
Or any other name it's known by

Doctor King would be upset by the crime
It wasn't for that he fought so hard

Gray   the suicide shade of northern weather
A climate one sets against hour-by-hour
    when even the color of one's cheeks is helpful

What's left of autumn's not enough rouge
South Genessee Street sounding almost Italian

After Harry's kindness   turn on the headlights
And perhaps that minimal technology
    will be all that's necessary
        to see your way in the day
                that isn't really that

See those planes?
They don't look built

      its more they're conjured   and put on display

Where is the Boeings "roar"?
The engines being tested?
They're someone's Christmas presents
                      ahead of schedule
                  model planes
       so close to the real thing
       they could fly like real planes
                      and be hijacked, even

It's Mister Short's neighborhood
The marine who'd become a piano teacher
    my very own
It's the land of piano lessons and recitals

Halfway up the Lakeside hill
       the home he made for *all* of us
We'd see his wife now and then
              emphatic!
            approving!
Applauding those short piano pieces
       that sounded across the tilted lawn
       applauding our not giving up!

Renton High School is over there
Like a seminary of teens
       praying their way through puberty
       stress that requires Bruckner to relive

Behold!
The grassy field of ground balls and pop-ups
        all uncatchable!

Bruckner and clouds
German clouds
       come all the way from Europe
      in support of the composer
           his many repeats   and crescendi

The symphony's going well, indeed
There's a U-Haul there on the right

grateful for such a powerful send-off
                                everyone moved!

Why not turn and see the haven house again?
Where you and your best friend would meet
      and Connie   his grandmother
           would act the part of Mae West
           and mimic others too
Her husband Henry was always game for a part to play

Why not view
      if even for a moment
          the happy verandah
          where Gary and I
          would youthfully philosophize

Like amateur Greeks we were
      in our outdoor classroom
      two friends
          very determined
              to get to the bottom of things

Gary   who always looked the same
The same at sixty
      as he had in the sixth grade playground
      when we swore allegiance

Perhaps it was the work of the control tower
Raised to supervise affections
                    ensure they last

The capillary branches
      like a barren avenue of Versailles
      that's surrendered to internal combustion

Airport Way is barely drivable
The entire town has gotten ahead of itself
        the streets not to be trusted, exactly
The lanes are plain but the year is not
            and phases in and out of relevance

Red-and-white checkered wall   a barrier

Memorial to many car races with no clear winners
The white dimples' bumps barely control the traffic

I may have to park and walk
    the better to imagine the long-ago night school
        that must be a day school by now
My father's effort to better himself
    before the family lost interest

It was a Boeing building like a barracks
But the "army" didn't want him
It wasn't he didn't belong
    it was more,
        "Dad! don't go drinking, okay?"

It's okay, though
    close to a first down
    close enough for jazz
Dad, I won't pick on you
    the universe simply unfolds
    and fear is just a part of it

Get off his Airport Way
The way he went
    to be all he could be in the Boeing military
The *best* jig maker!
And he can't have a whiskey when it's over?
                  why *not?*

Let's see Garden Avenue North
    whose Sartori Elementary is
        and has been
            since, hey, 1939
A "duck-and-cover" place
Fourth grade itself more dangerous than bombs
    so that first
        then second   and third   were effortless

There were those wonderful occasions, however
When the kindly
    the motherly   fourth grade teacher
                 read to us from "Huck Finn"

She would have the right idea
                    at the very right time

"Just put your books away, my darlings, and listen!"
Better than the monkey bars!

It was mostly Gary and I
Sometimes the music teacher would have us sing
    American folk songs
        "The Wabash Cannonball" was one
He made me play tunes I didn't like on the piano
        "The Wedding of the Painted Doll"

Was it "Sar" or "Sat", Satori?
The school that sounds like a meditation
                      was the meditation
Say "Sartori"
       and enter those halls with the waxy floors
       and hear the sounds of many shoes' ricochets

Meadow Avenue   Garden   Meadow
How bucolic!
       but there'd once been a foundry   pounding
Made quite a racket in Renton
Not much of a garden then   or meadow

Still   the shrubberies stood   and the maples
It was a noisy kind of Eden
No sex as yet
      only dogs and cats
         and ducks in the glades

Why do childhood homes seem small?
When the future comes they're scaled back

With E.T.A. Hoffmann waving his wand
      Meadow Avenue North
         that was once simply Meadow Street
The new name more specific
     understandable   informative

Additional knowledge
    of a place
        where pale blue down-sized house
            had somehow remained
            the third and last address we knew

And others
    the very white house
                        with the old square columns
Figment of the classical
        cut loose to be a chaste anomaly

The Holmas' tapered barn
Remodeled   remade
        from all the ghost-gray flecks   and peeling

Drive it slowly, of course
As if it were the Moon
        where you don't get out of the Lunar Rover
            without life support
                being a stranger
And it's all so long ago it's First Contact
Any EVA to be limited

A neighborhood with bungalows
Kick-the-can streets in that same one-way future
Two-way lost to convenience
        as it's really the night
            and the sky's a white lie

There should be limb shadows shifting
    with the street lights' power to render contrast
    when the Renton winds arise
                and twist the branches 'round

And where the Meadow ends   notice
        the great blankness
            where the foundry   rested   rusted
                            and was gone

Funny how the turning point
    for a sentimental journey

            becomes a certain lakeside to see
Kennydale Beach
    which
      if remembered
      if found
          would be the best of all changes of direction

It is already that   just being thought of
But search for it slowly
      taking Sunset Boulevard awhile
          the gradual ascent of it
          before less gradual Seventh Avenue
Enjoy the twists
            and the way no sunset was really required

For the west   from there
      resembled nothing the sun would want to visit
              and certainly over and over

Drive on
Take time to recall
      the road had been the path to a library job

And once   while walking it
      there came the thought
          that each step was sufficient achievement
Didn't stick to it though

It was called the "Permanent Highlands" then
Because we'd moved there
      from the other, just plain "Highlands"?
How high, anyway?
Three hundred feet above the "Lowlands" perhaps?

The ice had been here
A lobe of it right down Puget Sound   and grinding
Now the land is car-strewn
      SUVs in place of glacial erratics   the older models

Each Douglas fir is believing in solitaire

Dayton   the nice-sounding avenue

One of the curvy ones
    Dayton that crosses Edmonds
  and will take you to the second house
      if you want   and you do want that

Off of Edmonds see the second house we knew
Like a ranger station for a playground sandpit
                          headquarters

There should have been brochures
      for "Swiss Cheese Mountain"
        dug with tablespoons and time on our hands
Some pamphlet for "Mount Cliffly Flat Horn" too
    telling routes
        and where the best jump-off spots were
            for a tumble down the clay sand

Second house
We'd make of it sometimes a ship at sea
    or write music with our fingers
        on its steamed-up window panes

Keep going   you're not done

Seek H Street   called Harrington now
And stay on that till the *first* house appears
      and the same trees as then
        that were so scary in windstorms

Call it Mercury Way instead
For once you'd walked it
      sure the element had poisoned
The class that day had been "quicksilver"
you'd touched it by accident
    walked home   morose
    sure you would die

Highland Elementary's so much more than that
A happy blue it *is*   and vast

There's the old fire station
        become an auto care place

Same bricks   different century

Orrin Black   Highlands pal
Where *exactly* did you live?
Which of these boxes was yours?
Wasn't there an exceptional tree next to it?
    a Douglas fir   somehow moral   yes
    and if concertized the wind
        a sussurus so pleasing!

At some point the sound would begin to believe in itself
    and be not dependent branches
        but roar with prehistoric meaning
        solitaire
Orrin and I would listen
The tree   a chapter from a cautionary tale
        told with raindrops' punctuation

Shock of the New!
Those light lime apartments stacked
    like a land-locked cruise ship's superstructure
    among mere boats of Fifties antiquity
        the houses we lived in
            with *Nutcracker* furnishings

H Street   a long one   Harrington
Long as the G Note Road of Paderewski
    minueting every mystery of youth
        a presentation   which steps to begin
        but it's a riddle
If you were thinking of solving it   be dissuaded

Hopefully the first house is there
Its sixty-two years standing   hopefully
    for a great blank space attests to revision
        the Highlands "marina" swept aside
            for yet another grade school
                ghosted with bygone Boeing families

It *is* still there!   first house
Where Northeast Sixteenth Street is
            its lawn a parking place

I am so glad it's windy for this reconnaissance
And a very red car across the way
       is welcome counterpoint
             to the black-and-white mind
                   busy
                   so busy
                   with remembrance

I have not done badly
Haven't tried to drag the location away
      am simply content with the "contact-high"
         not wishing to possess it, really
           the whole neighborhood under the influence

First house
      from which excursions were made
         to as much discovery as the Highlands afforded
First house   that was the destination that first day
                          in July of 1951

And   careful so as not to attract attention
         do get out of the car
         and consider the corner
             where the only fight happened
The one-time fist fight
When you   belligerant   premeditating
      took on a bully as champion of the weak

Though who was weak and specifically abused
That is now unclear

Consider the school on the hill
We'd watched it being built
      playing in the construction ditches
          hiding too in the fresh lumber assembled

And remember always rain
Rain in the gutters and drains
Rain sounding on the roof   or pushing under doors

Storms that frightened more than eastern hurricanes

      but provided for play dams
              and other watery diversions

Recall the damp stumps of the further forests
   near to the valley
     where the towers draped their lines
         in a swath of clearing

Terrain where we steeply would descend
Slipping in the ferns and wet leaves
Slipping into *nirvana's* simplicity
   descent and ascent repeated
     those yards of deepness
        profoundly explored
          and respected

It was odd   how   seeing it now
   this place of *kinderscenen*
     again it seems just an earlier-in-the-day thing
     a region of marbles

So the search for Kennydale included diversion
I play in these streets again
   being here is all that's required

Playing as *then*
   with so much time
     weeks may pass
       between breakfast and lunch
The psychedelic trance that drugs attempt
   with wink-wink and nod-nod
   and nothing but insanity
     to *this*
     the power of bliss!

And it cancels slavery   and prison
Every Ought and Should ever proposed by grown-ups

Kennydale's down the hill
The rolling road
   after Edmonds runs out of room at Devil's Elbow
     and veers   down

as Northeast 27th Street

Is it familiar?
Really?
Was it ever?

Downward over the freeway's gash
                          to the highway at Washington
The first president got a lake
     with an island too
           expensive Mercer
           exclusive Mercer
The great mystery of monster mansions and giants
Over there

There's a Kennydale left
The beach has been spared
     and even those train tracks
       you'd look both ways for an engine
       the tracks are part of getting there
          always were
       but dangerous only in principle

The bright slides and swings have no sharp edges
And their candy colors are untasted hallucinations
Something intensely added to browns
                            and dark green
        seeing no use at all
         but their splendor's *acceptable* clutter
        filling in the plain beach

The little dock remains
     and kennydale's dimensions
         all of it sunburning
            the overcast deceptive as always

Do not swim beyond the boundary flotation
     that cozies the lake so otherwise vast
Philosophy of "less is better"
It was mother lake
     the whole Cosmos out there
         certainly over one's head

And you can't touch the bottom
    that was such a reassuring muck

Done?   hardly!
Too many nuts and bolts to sort
        summers to grasp

Though there isn't a law
    this idyll is breaking-and-entering Youth
    and successful burglary   for the moment

Harry got a call from me
But Kennydale's been ringing itself off the hook
    saying, "Pick up! Pick up!"
    yet I cannot answer
Better not to know what it wants
        probably a lot more than brunch

I should reenter the afternoon
    slip into a freeway's directional flow
        join others on their way to an Interstate

It's over   soft sand and tiny shovels
At least until a lottery's winnings
    overwhelmingly purchase the patch of this shore
    and the arrow of time is made to spin

The little bears on the dash
    have had enough of poverty
We'll travel, yes!
We'll go back!
Look, bears!
    I'm starting the engine   and starting *back*

Found the nearest star in coming, though

Return to the coastal tether of south and north
    drawn taut
        with day and night   together spliced
        and wanting only a *worthy* clock
Let the headlights be a scrutiny   lend "Adieu"

And drifting south on 5
    think the flooded plain
        near to Lacy
            a relevant metaphor
How easy it is to drown those acres
        where small trees are a surprising immersion

Exit 111   for those in love with boggy pastures
For the curious
    who wonder
        whether salt or fresh water comprised the inlet
            strange in blue twilight

There's a way to Port Townsend, too
The loop of 101
        how it follows the edge of the Olympics 'round
            staying coastal
                shores of the Sound
                of the Strait
                of the Pacific

Another day, though
For now   apologize to this highway
    for it's been begging
        "Know *all* of me for once!   turn right!"

But you don't
Because the site of Bruceport's more important
A vanished port that can be a story
        not knowing any actual details
Make imaginary the place
            so that we enjoy alternate history
                half-in and half-out of the day
                              what do you say?

Let's add to the coast concept
Add what is beyond the favorite six-part map
      include Raymond, even
      my brother-in-law's town
      Raymond just this once
The inclusion to be exceptional of course

That makes it all right
Don't be afraid to do it
Don't think it's a bad idea
    just because a brother-in-law doesn't like you

Raymond's later
Close in on Montesano first
    thinking Italian for awhile

Go easy
    the blackness Saturday
        at five-thirty
            gives it unity
Montesano's of one mind to disturb the universe

Elma's involved as well
The two towns a double threat in the dark
Talk to your sweetie against a background of menace
She will speak with a voice of a place
    where the sea has made a shell
                of solid stone

Talk with her
    seventy-five miles north of Astoria
She will want a summary
Perhaps when you're asleep behind the wheel
        with an expectation of deer at any time

An expectation a deer will jump   inexplicably
Being awake is no guarantee you won't collide
It's their nature to leap
    to be in the way   they jump anywhere
        even in the cities

Raymond's a city with those steel cutouts
    animals fixed
        that stay in place
            as rusted silhouettes   deer and more
And the art of cutouts everywhere

Raymond   closer to the sea than I thought

Because   whenever "Raymond" was heard
    so was a form described as inland situated
        animals
        chores
        errands

Raymond's town *and* country then
Closer to the sea than I ever imagined
                imagining Raymond

Weyerhausen   the company
When Mount St. Helens blew   Weherhausen lost
They owned the Land of Ashes
    their sticks of blown-down timber

But in the absence of volcano-love
    trees of all sizes and ages
        unnatural   the old-growth refugia
Islands surrounded by the mono-culture of seedlings

An edition of the land
    that also includes
        the recently harvested
           tortured terrain   of chaotic roots and stumps
                strewn

This is not a censure
If it were
    I should have climbed into the crowns of trees
    and made houses up there in defiance
        causing delays
The chosen trees given a little more time
                to be unfelled

What will you do?
Out here in the dark
    the coast is most like poetry attempted
        as it is most conceptual then

And   being invisible
    the forest   and all else there is
    the night is better assembled and understood

Cross a creek on 101
    knowing that intersection with a watershed
        is a hope that more will be revealed
Who lives in the homely dwelling
                minimally illumined
And how soon it will be they have an open house
                      in the woods

Two dark figures on the bridge
Raymond   on the Willipa
Near to the city center
    seen beyond the dashboard bears
        that are eerily alive
        now that neon flashes
            it's obvious they *too* have a nightlife

Raymond after dark
And crossing a second bridge
    with a McDonalds glowing
        Raymond's written longhand   in stone
Cursive thought   and a *beguiling* script
Good penmanship   good citizenship
        not to mention what's moored in the harbor

South Bend
Just before leaving *that* town
    note the library's closed
        though it wants your books
        those written and those projected
Would add their titles   if there's time for that

Is there only a South Bend and not a North?
Don't beat yourself up finding out
The reading room awaits
    nocturnal study   the *art* of finding out

If there's an In-and-Out Burger   and there is
    let libraries copy and customers read
    really read   everything on the shelves
                checked In-and-Out

Until South Bend's absorbed
And all its authors made celebrities
I'll stay until it's done
    and date the librarian too

Until a red light turns to green in the country
It's roadwork   wait
So odd to see signals
    and no streets for them to govern

Wait   it's a one-way deal
You can do it   though impatience rules your life
    like a petty, wheezing tyrant
    always demanding knowledge
            of your whereabouts
    and where have been placed
           your most precious pyramids

Where!
That the tyrant
    like a vengeful god of art
        might smash them!

It's a perfect landscape
Even the bears are satisfied
    and set out plates for dinnertime berries

The color black is tutoring
Does not distinguish a hill from a dale
Wants mystery to matter most
    why I signed on in the first place

This part's moot
    but I need the dark to teach detail
    and it does   grudgingly
        trusting the pupil's mind to take a hint

As at Knappton   *two* "p's" mind you
Knappton more a ghost wharf
        its pier pegs orderly
           outlining

What's left is enough
The enterprise still is thriving
    whose poles remain
      and those extra bundles
        seen lashed like thick tipis

They must denote the ferry's dock
Where the boats bumped and fendered
          and then were made secure

Ferry to Astoria   which
    right now
      a distant horizontal carnival's line of lights
        lets you know the river has an edge
              at least one

This Knappton is the other   more spurious
It must have been the place you got to and from
      the cars floating on the Columbia
        low tide or high on its river-sea's miles

Wandering over   like a mind will do that
    still unmade-up
The bridge that replaced   like thought control
          like progress always is

Call it the Astoria-Megler Bridge
Though believe it's Knappton the ferry went from
      and would come back to
        in an approximate way
          without headlights and head-on's

Can someone say what the sandbars mean?
Those mid-river   and seeming permanent, too
Say why it is
    there is no depth where one expects it
      the river's center line a shallow thing
            pier poles, even

As though the Columbia's prodigious lecture and flood
    missed the main point

                was proven wrong
                and survived through watery tenure alone

Good to be across its untrustworthy premise
Astoria   though incomprehensible itself
                        seems a lesser enigma
Drive its methamphetamine streets
        drawing no conclusions whatever

Warrenton   Fred Meyer
The guy's everywhere
                like John Jacob Astor

Ross is here
You "dress for less" but never leave home
Such are the chains you stay in one place
                and do not travel anywhere at all

Rite Aid   anyone sure of that?   that it's right?

What are all these chains doing
                    in the land of Lewis and Clark?
Is it really just eight miles to Seaside?
Or is Cyber World just fooling around?
There's a robot voice: "Get *in* here!"
    the robot itself then appears
        I must do what says
            and seek Aid within its aisles
                    brightly fluorescent!

In the Tsunami Hazard Zone
    the sign's a pretty blue-and-white
It depicts in sign language
Waves of increasing height
    and an Everyman attempting to elude them

His posture is flight   articulated
The faceless stick figure
    appearing to clamber to safety
        to higher ground
            but   I don't know
            I think he's done for

I guess you'd feel the shaking   *considerable* shaking!
And it would last quite awhile, wouldn't it?
         for it would be the tremble of subduction

Don't know what that is?
Should know what that is!
            we live in the *World!*

Question is:
     does anybody really want to be that figure?
     does anyone really want to obey?

Hold that thought
     as one might hold one's breath
            with the commencement of all that shaking

The Great Wall Restaurant and Lounge
                         In the Tsunami Hazard Zone
And the U-Haul and the Windjammer Motel
            right there in the Tsunami Hazard Zone
And Gearhart Liquors, too   in the Tsunami Hazard Zone

Everybody's living   where?   right there
                         in the Tsunami Hazard Zone!
Wonder if the siren would sound the same as Japan's
And if the alarm's a standard wailing
     rising and falling with first alert

Something slightly World War in nature
Cousin of air raid   but different
     a slower oscillation
            its amplified range up-and-down
                              like the ocean

And the airport?   well
     the waves would come in for a landing there
Think of waves in the night
Waves like the ones that spilled in 1964
     all the way from Alaska
            while the moon turned searchlight

If one does not dawdle and stays on the road
    Kennydale down to the sea of jolts
        will cost a mere three hours and forty-five minutes

That's all
And that's enough evening
    to seem like a morning of death-by-drowning
    or any *other* death that says,
      "I'm done fooling around!
        and do not fear the Gateway!"

Gateway of Gearhart   Seaside   and more
Passing the Pizza Palace
    realize how meager is the appetite
        in the presence of philosophy

When the need for calories lessens
    and is no need at all
As though thought alone were sustenance
    if what's on your mind is sufficiently intriguing

Nothing in the night will frighten
There was Cesar Franck's *Nocturne* took care of that
The song   which
    in f sharp minor
      begins "O, belle nuit..."
        and continues to praise the darkness
          with four stanzas of French words
            sung to a sleepy piano

Stop-and-Go
    like convenience
      always open
        yet priceless
          the clerk dozing off
Semi-enchanted so that commerce knows an itermission
    under the spell of chromatic harmony

I am momentarily studying very hard
Self-enrolled in Clatsop's Community College
Learning by osmosis   in the night of your music, Cesar

Knowledge imparted
The brain putting new ruminations to bed

Oceanography and marine biology absorbed
    acted upon
      a show playing   with science the feature attraction
Diamond Heating insures you stay warm for the semester

There's a theater for all this
The admission is your own thesis
    and wondering expressed
You see a movie of a journey
Reel-to-reel with no interruptions
        an Adidas "check" mark
        for every scene change

There's a store called Carter's
It's all about babies and kids
    wonderful!   all that attention paid!

Osh-kosh Jones   New York
Some outlet to go with inlet
    the *very* big city
      come to the country
      to make sophisticate the boonies

It's a long stretch of retail
    and strip malls make their case for distraction
    with endless windows and logos

Slip past Necanicum   where it flows south to north
Always somehow overdue
    as if it did not wish that mixing with seawater
The smoothie to be delayed by languid pools
As Seaside settles in for the night
    and Cannon Beach begins to turn down its covers

Let us see that whale again   sculpted   representing
The whale at Ecola Creek
The model cetacean
    that celebrates the whale ashore the Indians found
    and then told to the Corps of Discovery

                which came to see
            well   a few of them
                including Sacajawea, yes

They came too late
Too late to find more than bones to admire
But there it had been
        a diversion
            an excuse to cross over Tillamook Head
                and see beyond immediate concerns

The monolith that would later be known as Haystack
        and other   more distant   rocks   islands
            the Castle

All this they would have seen
For the first time
        and / will see things for the first time, too
            in finding the sculpture

So use the bridge into Cannon
That which replaced the weaker one
                            wave-smashed in '64

Zigzag the blocks
Ninety degrees of left and right
        at 8:15   post meridian
                November 15th, Saturday
Passing the Rotisserie Lumberyard
                a good place to dine

Then   the flashlight   shine it on the whale
It's found in the park
        small   memorial stone and more
            one of the evening's many alcoves

Be out of the car with that flashlight
And go to it   immobile as legend

You are safe from highways
        and the challenge of lane changes   signals
            speed down to a quarter mile-an-hour

Quite slow to-and-from the whale
Dead-idle in its presence

Play the flashlight over it
A whale that reflects   gleams
     its flukes a graceful bronze
And if it's *not* that metal yet say it is
Just once
     close enough for jazz
       and wanting history back for the sake of beginnings

Perhaps in the night   it is an easier acrobat
Summoning the chosen image
     the l.e.d. an effortless enlightenment
       here   there
         the entire whale inferred from several sweeps
Discrete yet adding up to mammal

Unteachable are its songs   and all their scan
Unthinkable the factory ship on the horizon
     one of God's fine days of azure

For a moment it's Burning Man
     though why that should be eludes

Love of the night out there
Finding love right here in the shadows
Night that is elevated
       like a host

Night that sends envoys   imaginings
That is inclined to silence
     and returns us to less-demanding midnight psalms
How the absence of one sight heightens the others

The whale is dimly inspected
     as if it were undersea
     and viewed from a bathyscape
         Jacques Costeau advising

The whale deep down in a dive
     the way Cannon Beach inhabits the subconscious

      and is the maker of strange dreams
In the court of Poseidon the sea god threatens,
With his trident he gestures
He will withdraw his favors
        if I should stay away too long
          but it doesn't really work that way

He comes to me   and always has
There was never any other arrangement

Play the flashlight again   the whale body to discern
Dully illumined
    as though not wishing to be seen
        in this condition of cold blood
        and arrested migration

I had to promise to go in its stead
            to any depth he should assign

I was involved
My father had always said to study hard
            to study science
There'd be a lot of catching up to do in one night's vigil

The sea's white noise near
Official as the word's onamatapojea
    the endless sound
      unless the ocean is becalmed
        and made a vast and waveless lake
          as sometimes happens
            and surprisingly

There is no repose this evening, however
And the surf is motion
    as much as *ecola* is perfectly still with divorce
You drink from the fountain prior to departure

But you only go next door
To the historical site
The Cannon Beach Necanicum Salt Water swimming pool
                heated
    a beach front venture

in the pre-Depression year of 1924
It lasted till '41
Pearl Harbor a possible factor
William J. Mahone in charge
        did he serve?
        did he disappear?

Now it's simply called "Beachfront"
    the facade a churchly design
       perhaps a mission
            it's windows full of warm orange light

Two of those windows nicely slatted
Shatter-proof   against the demonstrations of beggars
    in some future apocalypse

The rest is alabaster molding
      graceful   optimistic
         as though architecture might appease
           the masses always impatient

There's a cross positioned
     between the doors
        oddly dark
          like an afterthought of faith
More the letter "T"   as an entire novel

"T" for "teach me"
"T" standing in for chapters and verses.
Dark cross inconspicuous
     as stolen happiness
           found or lost

Swim in the absent pool of it
Necanicum like a blessing
    the syllables trustworthy delirium
Swim *retrospectively* the pool
           and the chapel that replaced it

William J. Mahone
Is there a "y" to the surname?

An Irish catholic   connecting
    so that Christ went from wet to dry sanctuary
        making even more history?

The town is empty for this early
And the orange interior's taking no chances
    on further make-overs
        and by its Halloween glow
        tells of yearlong consolation

Before Acadia Beach is the Jockey Cap
There's a turnout there
    where Gary had come to see his best friend's beach
    see what all the fuss had been about
    for I'd raved
        trying to describe it
The complex of sea and shore   so much obsession!

After years and years
    we parked him in sight of it all
And he heard tell of the Cap and other wonders
The rock that looked like a jockey's headgear
    that was unclimbable
        but its smaller neighbor was doable

He heard of that adventure and more
What was found in the Starfish cave
How clambering there was like an invasion
                by an invasive species

Gary had been impressed
    maybe a contact high
        because I was still rhapsodizing   and pointing

There is a moon right now
Demonstrably benign
An eastern moon preparing a seascape
    one that will summon pearls to the beach
        and somehow infer their beauty
                from shades of gray

Ascend into the tunnel after Arch Cape's sign

Tunnel that has everything
    a rock wall
    a cement wall
        and Bruckner's Seventh
            immensely sounding!

Tunnel that is *concentrated* coming and going
Through the actual Cape
Getting inside its head
    trafficking human thought
        wishing no end to it
        as long as it is recreational

So bright in there
    let's just say it's daytime
The fact the lights are on means civilization
        some version of it
        resting on this accomplishment

A success of between-the-wars
The fact the walls are intermittant
            lets the mountain breathe
            shows what it's made of
            the bore *not* boring

Its abstract space is intervallic
The length of geometric rounding
    the accelerator pressed
        so that the tunnel's a gun
        and yourself   spent ammunition
        for a cannon's worth of mayhem and begone

Be Christ's crutch after Calvary
Where   in an alternative universe
    His crucifixion's interrupted
        and He limps away to be out of earshot
        and ask His Father,
            "What's going on?"

The sacriligious car is to blame
In the Arch Cape tunnel
    prepare to receive the fantasia

       that attends the hybrid's operation
The mind has a machine   or the driver's incorporate
      part of things
         more hybrid
          than the car alone can manage

Falcon Cove
Cove Road
    something exciting happened down there
    when we were roaming
       among the stones
         the large cobbles' jumble of well-rounded
           sun-warmed
            each heavy disc

No one will stop you from returning
No one has the time
Even if it seems like a good idea
    no one

That a creature should know such enjoyment in the cove!
Jealousy!   but no very bad behavior triggered
    in one on the lookout for happiness
    and wishing to destroy it

The placid sign like a dream's guideline
"This way go"
    to be among evening boulders
       handled heavily one-at-a-time
              close to the roar

That Moon walking day-for-night visibility
I'll be honest: the Light and the Dark have joined
    and it is a third condition

Like a very thin past
    that is neither Then or Now
       but the essence of In-Between
          which denies the Future its tense entirely

Is it ignorance or truth
      the middle of the night is safest terrain?

Ascending into the tunnel back there
                it seemed obvious
                   and is more so past the Cove

And coming to Necarney Creek
    explore it   pristine
        how much light is really needed?
"Necarney" some tribe
Or a tribe's term for a long-ago ghost

And no one will demand why you thrash
     trailblaze the underbrush   the understory
    writing just that: an Under Story
No one at all

Sooner disturb a deer in the night
Make an issue of its foraging
        why *this* place?
         that?

The Cyclops flashlight put to good use
    looking for all things lost
    even good penmanship
    that *too* in Necarney
        on the way to Neahkahnie

The mountain been to so many times
    the basalt surrendered
        told all there was to tell of Miocene time
Even estimating one's chances of enduring the sulphur

It is sport to elicit the landscape's longer ages
With accents strange the main events are told
The dramas so far apart
    that disbelief hovers over the narrative
    and all through the homeless eons
      with records being broken
      Nature stays angry enough
      to stowaway in our good times
Lying in wait for hubris

Those meadows like intelligence

spread out in the presence of hippie hermits
who divorced the crowd to make lean-to's
and think about the world as a whole

Neahkohnie
Spell it any way you want
We just want to hear you say it   that's all
and all of us will note
how the proper name
restores faith in language
to say a thing with sound alone

Neahkahnie
A way of life discredited
There is all the more yearning
in the letters
each proposing sadness should enter the alphabet
The word thus made

At the stone wall
know a probation
and increased pressure to stay on the road
given all that height above the sea
The Moon-Sun enough
to suggest a vertical highway's also possible

It would take some time to recover the Hybrid
Amidst pillars and skulls of some Manhattan deceit
Neahkahie is final
no plans

More "N's"   Nehalem now   there have been so many
Old and quaint on a human scale
Be a part of it
be a local for the length of the main drag
whose Food Mart will stay unrobbed
by me and you combined

It would be so unacceptable

What music for Nehalem?
What cd of fifteen seconds

        to accompany that right turn to the water
          enjoying the well-lit Holocene
The Big Picture taken in a very small town

And where you curve around   and carefully
     the name is a river
        the Nehalem
          leaking out of higher horizons
                  than the sea proposes

Millions of Baby Boomers
      pushed aside for the sake of inlet
           and insightful monologue

Or it's the model for orderly succession
Perceived in headlights' haphazard assignment
"Please believe in me!"
      the river again
"Believe and belong the way *I* do!"

You're going over an opportunity for sure
     curving around
      as if *coming* around, perhaps
Baby in a bath of miles
       sold on maturity
         while still in diapers   plural

The curve   a change of habit
One-upping humdrum
Didn't I say it was easier in the dark?

Want to talk about Wheeler?   / will
That old town of Wheeler back there?
     well, it had an Old Wheeler Hotel
        that won't bother anyone determined
                    to pass it by

Anything *truly* old around here is hard to find, however

This is one story of what went on in that hotel
It was the summer of 1963
    when the hotel was not so old

Back when guys' ties were skinny
And a president could be Left and Right *both*
    and have as many affairs as back pain permitted

Susan came to stay   and stay
She stayed so long it was home at last
She'd wanted a place to be
    where she might decide on something important
        but Wheeler got to be *more* important

Her daily walks filled in the blanks
    until complete thoughts were all that mattered
And so it was she realized everything by chance
        and made no decision at all
The Wheeler Hotel's boards and beds
So convenient a cat could have planned it
Stuff went on you might intuit
    a hundred years

There was a man named Henry
    who had a son, "Henry the Second" called
And on that son's birthday
    he was brought to the seashore
        December 19th, 1922

The second story   a special pre-Christmas present
Fishing out of Wheeler
    but the Second.Henry had other ideas
        said he'd rather write
        make it a writer's retreat

"Please, father   I appreciate your gift   but
    can it be the pen
        and paper of Old Wheeler Hotel stationery
        the window   and this wintry day?"

And so was a novel started   and stopped
    in the New Year   to critical acclaim
        thanks to good parenting

Third story   this very night
Amazingly, Victoria appeared

    in the heart of the weekend
    out of town and waving at the entrance

Her presence synchronicity itself
As I'd just thought of her
    performing at the Bottom of the Hill   San Francisco
Thought of her en route

And so a third story may be told
How both of us
    far from home
    found out the waking hours
        were just a very bright evening

We were rapartee and stylish rejoinders
Promenading until the entire town took notice
    those still up-and-running anyway

It was the Old Wheeler
    spinning more and more history
        with a hundred years to back it up

Victoria had surprised
    and wrote new songs in the old hotel

"Better get ahead and not behind," someone said
    overheard
        was it advice   or agreement?

Victoria Victrola
    her hat aslant
Victoria singing of Vancover Island
    her name a city's identity
        when a ship called the *Princess Marguerite*
          would depart Seattle on the windy Sound
        to go there   and often

Yet the beautiful singer was an illusion
A trick played by circumstance

Suffice to say she *could* have been there
Checked in   perhaps preparing for a gig

just thinking of her
the Day-for-Night coast did gift the apparition
assembled her features from enchantment
It was a great kindness shown

Let us Rockaway
And raise concerns about demonization

By nine-o'clock parted to reunite south
We both live musical lives
and the keyboard's our very good friend

The *town* of Rockaway like a philosophy of separation
Lake Lytle a resplendant puddle
near to the Surfside Resort
a conservative concept awaiting adherents

Say "Rockaway"
and everything you love about the ocean's known
Rockaway Beach containing its sound
and summoning the artists

It's not easy to get here
Don't think of highway miles
Rather   imagine "here"
as the peace you want
rocking   slowing
a radio maybe
And what you say stays said   and not denied

The black beauty of the lake
held   just barely
its own standards met

There's a strange sign seen   undecipherable
It's been over and over seen
for quite a while, really

It seems a depiction
Haystack Rock as logo   but that cannot be
The Haystack shape has a hidden meaning

A symbol newly arrived in some sense
The sign stays a tease
    like, "My country, 'tis of thee..."
    though my country is New Guinea

"Be not troubled"

It was advice given in Twin Rocks
Place that needs a narrative   back from Limbo
Needs that story of a man and his wife reunited
    one day of
        "I know what you know
        let's be in love again"

That Limbo that's a lost location
    the place a story can get to
I was careless
    and mourn the specific pages stolen

Twin Rocks will be remembered appoximately
Imagine a return   a story returned
    Twin Rocks making a marriage new

Imagine a stay
    what further reconnaissance might uncover
The couple stays apart till then   best advice

And a recurring sign unparsed
            a cryptic Burma Shave

Franck's *Beatitudes* eases the mystery
            into acceptable quandary
        his soloists and choirs
        going to be good company

Marylyn's Home-Style   Away-Style, too
But do we have enough *Income* for Marylyn?!
The lottery's stayed elusive as kangaroos
    and   jumps away from the chosen numerals

Oh, lottery!
How many flirtations you're responsible for!

shocking, really!

Barview will keep its jetty for now
    while I,   like a dwelling   am riprapped
The actual *view* from the bar   uncertain vision
You fill in the blank scenery with earnest fantasias
    that spin off of Cesar August
        his musical checks and balances

Drive with care
    to hear the end of the oratorio
        with those last   organ-embellished measures

Marylyn   who sang for the president's birthday
    blondly inclines to the counterpoint
        happy to depart from pop values for awhile

Relationship   an account   Marylyn and Joe
They would visit the Hotel Utah bar
    in San Francisco   after games
And she'd had a favorite seat
One where she could not see herself in the bar mirror

Yeah   relate to that
As if fame would always have nothing to do
        with who was famous
      and be tangent at best
      be beyond the life that was lived

And Joe might have said, "Come closer"
    those times she retreated from the stars
    and was simply demure
        homespun
          Barview

And there are four sandstone platforms
    that come with tip-of-the-tongue names
So they are not only dimly apprehended
        but vaguely pronounced
       barely titled
They lurk behind the eyelids' flutter
Elusive as the nighttime's light

A museum's walls tested for darkness
A curator challenged
    by an artist able to paint the night
    or take its picture in such a way
        though it be broad daylight
            yet would the museum goer go to sleep

The artwork spectral   nocturnal
The same as the apparitional stacks
            with briefest topknot foliage
      open-air closet space
      stubby   dense

"The Four Graces"   *that's* what they're called!
Miniatures imbued with personhood   assigned them
State of remainder
    like geological math proposed
        and erosion's a respectable sculptor

Their silhouettes converge
    and for a moment join
        for my transit of the bay's fringe flats
Dark Russian dolls encased in the *single* mother shell
One sculpture

I'm alive with perspective
    and race the engine a little   prior to going

Remember the day they were climbed on
I was a toy soldier
    trying to be a smaller army of one clay figure
    for whom the towers were immensities

What is remembered will have edition
                        before we have done
           Garibaldi
            town not known
      little city with that "G" on the hill
        that "G" lit up and golden
the sixth letter of the alphabet
    smitten by all the attention paid

As the marine fish known as the "lookdown" looks down
So am I gazing   a land fish   the *other* way
    thinking
        if there isn't a God
        the "G" can serve
        and is a close enough capital
                    to furnish blessings

The letter *high* enough for that
        and gilded   as heaven is
It's all you could ask for   so very frazzled
                    off-the-path and erroneous
A sign   and rescue as good as the Coast Guard
keeping it secular
        though you may be entitled to more

Garibaldi's cannon
The left-over chimney
        prepares a salvo
            the dark blasting the Dark

It is entropy's preview
And whatever factory it was had its industry stolen
Whatever the funnel was a part of
            pales   now it's artillery

New usage   non-commercial
The furnace place at the base is cold
        and coldly does the smokestack fire
        a great cylinder's worth
                    of doubt and reservation

Though its aim is off
    and the "G" is safe
        it is *blatant* affront   symbolic
The planet turns with satisfaction
    so much is going on
            by way of protest
                in Garibaldi

What must the cities be up to, then?

This will be a new book
    about Italy   its founder's town
  tightly constructed
      like a good constitution

And the rain that comes to Garibaldi
    is dark poetry of yet another nation
Sleep on it
Sleep on the "G" as well
The next planet needs this consonant too
              and Puccini to serenade

Tillamook   the highway splits
    downtown
    the arrows unmistakable

After the cheese factory palace
      where there's not one way to do things

After the big box   that was like a dairy's apotheosis
    and cow's perfectability
    the goal of all that grazing and mooing
Where tours are taken and amazement ensues

After intuiting a swing shift's boredom
Enjoy the all-lit-up center of town
    its dragstrip potential to rival *American Graffiti*

There is the road to Netarts and Oceanside
Karen's coast   Oceanside
    place where a bee got in the car one time
    that Oceanside

And just saying, "Netarts", by day or night
    is being there
Netarts   not a plural, really
Netarts as quintessential seaside
    the name sounding somehow exactly right
              for that strand

Fight back against a schedule!
You want to go there again and risk a bee yourself

But not this time
There's a course
    and a weekend *only*
        Friday/Monday brackets
        the bookends of a coastal library

Love your home again
Both *this* home of driving
        and the home base of rehab

It is now one mile to Three Capes Loop
That's the one to take
    "Let's go further!" it says
      meander   stretch it out
        loop around   the To-and-From lengthening
        Meares!   Lookout!   and Kiwanda!
Won't take you *that* out of your way
But hell! *Be out of your way!*

It is an all-new desire to excel at being diverted
Being able to go to sleep amidst the "chains"
All the chains
    7-11   The Arches   the drug stores
    the food stores and Dollar's deals

As if nothing's wrong   not *really*   hah!
Deep breathing all that global warming
    the star keeping its date with future Earth

Old Tillamook's a matter of simply straight ahead
The Oregon Coast Dance Theater
    the Timeout Tavern
        The Dutch Mill Cafe   (park in back)
        Tangled Yarns
           a movie theater still in business
What the A-Bombs missed

But never mind fission
Why is it no battles have ever been fought here?
Here in the bottomlands
    where the five rivers flow
        and numerous sloughs are back-and-forth

There were no causes?
No religions contending?
Guess not
    guess Tillamook's unusual, then
    the townsfolk so used to peace
        they indulge in sleepwalking all day long
        the waking dream a *communal* experience

The theater now showing how it's done

The crosswalks resemble the one on that Beatles album
    the four of them walking
        the chalk-white segments emphasising separation
        discretion
            each musician "underlined"
        liable to split
Leave the band at any time

Tillamook's avenues
    streets and boulevards
        telling time away
        and what can't be seen
Until a reckoning is possible
And lost art retrieved before the dawn

What I wanted to express the most of all
The indirect moonlight such
    the color grey is asked to do too much
    is called on over and over
        diffusing silhouettes
            grey-entitled

At the turnoff to Munson Falls
    and Pleasant Valley experiences total recall
The sky is a soft computer
Rounding off the numbers of its nocturne
    even as Chopin assists at his Pleyel
                Edgar Allen Poe turning pages

Best the satellite's unseen
Like the countryside

    knowing how much may be taken for granted
And sparse Douglas firs are *each* more sturdy then

Philosophy's light   filling in the empty meadows
To be this pleasant
       and still be blank
           attests to the best
              the cinematic mid-century could offer

The engine likes this stretch
And has settled into a different "hum" than so far
Rather a *mechanical* contentment
       wishing to include the driver, too
         albeit indirectly
As the Moon almost secretly illumines the hills
                         to the right of 101

Beyond   the improbable cyclist
    weighed down
      laboring dangerously
Trusting the cars will stay on the road

A death wish   roulette
He *should* be camped by now
      with the latest leg of the journey replaying
    as he falls asleep
All the day's details   spilling into p.m.'s finale
           seeing it safely with second sight
        a tour done twice and lucidly

I'll be generous like Harry
I'll pay for your KOA
     just don't be barely in the headlights
                      just be off the road

Valley Junction
Dead tavern   it's a Saturday night
   it sure is closed
     closed like a mind   to all but vacancy
What the hell is it called?
  Some bar-and-grill   definitely not happening
                     at all not happening

But wait a minute!
Hebo Inn   *that's* happening
            and the Hebo Market   open!

Wouldn't it be wonderfully strange
     to save Hebo *only* for the night?
       Only come to the Junction once the sun is down?

There was a long-ago time
     when a certain symphony of Dvorak
          the one in F major
               could only be played going to sleep
Could only be heard when a specific constellation shone
     having come 'round the sky
          to twinkle through the cherry tree

I called it "The Wizard of Oz" constellation
The whole concept takes too much explaining
Though the star maps say "Hercules"
     the guy with the club
          hey!   nothing doing!
          it was a starry map of Oz I saw

Four main stars   somewhat dim
A quandary of directions
     north   south   east and west
     the compass of Oz

Dvorak was the Wizard
Such a very fine symphony to sink into celeste
     you're asleep before it finishes

The junction here could use some emeralds, too
     and night vision
          to see the occasional hot air balloon
                              from the heartland

Not so fast!
Be in and out of Hebo's market
     to see what they eat in central Oz
          what table's set in Glinda's palace

What valley it is that's this valley alone
                          and Frank Baum's junction

I'll make you a proposal
      I'd be able to borrow enough money
           in the next ten minutes
                to rent a room at the Inn
             Proposal Rock Inn

The people are friendly in these parts
Take that bet
      my very own proposal we marry while we can
     our Neskowin honeymoon
           to include midnight snacks
                        in the sunken forest

Think it over   on the ascent south in the rain
The lone superpower's scenery
      the roadside trees like a cliff overhanging
Someone's directing   flawless
The entire cast agrees
          motionless
            though we certainly travel
                    upon a pointillist river

Is this Lincoln City?   this the one?
Still early enough to have traffic
      this city of five dollar bills
                city made of five others
            a fondue
        overlap and amalgamation

Good to have Abraham here in the west
     his name assigned to so many towns at once
         thousands of miles from Springfield
      his character suffusing

But *is* it Lincoln City?
Could it be?   I just don't know
     steeped in after-dark
     it seems a dream's teasings
And thinking so is all one can say

Keeping to the right lanes is all that's possible
It's enough, actually
      no drifting over
          and a "rat-tat-tat" of dimples down the middle
If a radical leftist were out here however
      there might be a head-on anyway

Long Lincoln is pouring
          out of a highway's vanishing point
         the way meteors will
            from a radiant sometimes
          shower down till dawn

But   *is* this Lincoln City?   by night?
Is it?
    I don't know

Like a car thief, *go!*
    map-ignorant
      Intent on defeating "Lo-Jack"
City unknown is all I can say

It could be   you know   drawn-out   run-on
City stretched   mobile
The entire population
    living on the couches of friends
    an elastic civilization
      small enough and large enough
        for all you want to do
          and you will be encouraged to do it

There's the Inn at Wicoma
I think it lies within the limits of Lincoln
Could a civil war get started?   States' Rights bruited?

I.G.A. Home Town
    very nice and very rebellious!
      the Cause goes on and on in the heart of Union
A mixture   imagine that!   well, okay

The superstore well-stocked

poverty's acquired the Econo-Lodge
and evicted the Republicans
and the Democrats
and every party that's ever been!

The infrastructure's no structure at all!
You must fall back on mythology
Get the story straight
see if you can parse the Indian legends
so that Lincoln's sequential
and adds up to what was

Let perpective follow
one to go with onrushing lights
Maxfield's at the coast doing very well indeed
And the movies shown in Lincoln City
show nothing ever seen before

It's really hard to say how this all got started
but the battles hereabouts are the easiest anywhere
and   significantly
there's plenty of morphine

When you see the signs for Devil's Lake
Hah!   at last you know how the movie will end
and confirmation's made
It is the sixteenth president's headquarters town

Though the bodies
at the bottom of the lake
will never vote   still
you get the feeling they'd support him

The trip to see Harry
was a truancy enhanced with teaching
And here   in the certainty that is Lincoln
crosshatched with benign
the city's streets tutor address
luck   and karma

They coach all the games of chance
that may still be played on folded boards

Christmas morning   noon   and night
In the aftermath of tinsel
     and its serene glitter
And Christmas has actually *started*
       if you count the colored windows
       already outlined
       and fences draped with l.e.d.'s

There is no mistaking that manger for a secular crib
And you wonder if that devil's been out and about
     and whether Lincoln's accommodations
       are adequate shelter
       from his scheming and cunning

He's more at large day-for-night   electric!
     in a false dawn shuffle
            hither and thither

Shearwater   stay *there*
Maybe out of harm's way
     where else?   maybe a luxury vacation home
Ah, yes!   if the devil should trouble you
A vacation home
     that's transferred from one person to another
     one *generation* to the next
       past judgment
       beyond weakness
           and fortified, even

You know, Van Gogh was the city planner
Planned those swirls   rain-soaked
     pressure on to apply the paint
       before his brush strokes no longer matter
The police will stay out of it
     the pictures stay unframed

As if there's shelter, though!
As if someone may truly be protected!
A million miles not enough safety
     to cease praying to the Buddha
     or keep opinions to oneself
       break down to base morality

At the West Shore Ocean Front you may seek succor
Beelzebub's shore
      he is the acting host since the manager's flight
          the dollars dried up
            and even barter is impossible

Remember to *do* something
      if the devil really bothers you
          don't just stand there!

Remember Depoe Bay and the short bridge over it
Remember young Stalin
      who walked with strange little steps
        as though Terror were precision
            monstrous as winter froth   whitely chaotic
        and the Russian state of Georgia
              an unbalanced state of mind

Odd   that a bridge may be built
              in either freedom or slavery
              and it holds up the same

Nature no help   proud of its beautiful neutrality!

Remove the boiler from Boiler Bay
Bring it back   and bring it to a boil
Been in the sea too long
      the corrosion unacceptable

Take it out of the ocean for repairs
      and place it in a brand-new boat
        Proving "old" is always relevant machinery
The past more than happy to be useful
            and explain everything

These coastal towns like ghostly overlays
A haunting
      where   what is most recently constructed
        is the most phantom for the two-by-fours

Get ready for more singing

Made-up songs the virgin mind imagines
    seated on the driftwood
    the more alive for dead timber
      and kelp bullwhips
          handled deftly   defiantly

The future like a seabird's cry
Purely causal   almost understood
The bird is mimicked
    and so closely it's avian ventriloquism
      yourself the willing understudy
      related to the dinosaurs *also*
      and passing the reptile's test for cold-blooded!

The ocean's well-illumined
    considering the absence of an actual moon
      that moon   dispersed   in the cumuli

And just *how* does an unseen moon manage
    to light an ocean even so
    the sun *most* indirectly shining then
      in this manner of moonburn
Ever so slightly
As if the center of the Solar System suffered censure

Or is it the world of Pluto beheld?
The surface receiving only the cold gaze
          of distant fusion
Pluto supplied with *our* ocean
    but it's a hard freeze in Space
      where Spencer Creek
        is through with falling downward
        and "least resistance" to its goal

It's God's truth
    that Seal Rock is eight hours from Kennydale's pier
The park's assemblage mostly profiles
Anthropomorphic   variations on a theme
          starkly realized

The one shape that conquers all
The masses experience separate conclusions

India's ink gone mad into it
    anger and violence   there in the shaping
       unsubdued
The Moon's pearls strewn with softest persuasions of grey

Grey enough for principal photography to start
At a director's signal
      though action's already underway

The rocks out there are anything you want them to be
In the uncertain light   a *menagerie* of seals
   colorless
    whiskered shades of charcoal
Prodigious   the lava hexagons a perfect puzzle fit

By the time the great blocks are broken down
Unjoined for reassembly
    the puzzle is no more

At Cape Perpetua
    after Yachats's uneven ledges
    and the mystery of Reeves Circle
Beware the bad basalt everywhere heaved!

There's a quietism
Sure of its powers to govern
    while it's raining around corners
                      and downhill, too

We must be courageous
    even if there are no obstacles
And the Hindu god in charge of removing them
     is an *idle* deity   albeit colorfully adorned

Oh, Perpetua!
    the woman whose name you received
       knows there is no finer headland!
In the medleys of nighttime radio
    her voice is heard
     and she interweaves Eternity
        while "pop" blasts its less lengthy forevers

And more rain's soft hail
    rattles Ford's Fusion
      and makes it a noisy submarine
          lauched from a berth in little Yachats town

It's possible to get to Florence
        sooner than you actually do
To be in Florence ahead of time
              the wheels still rolling to it
Anticipating Italy   right there in the headlights

I'm a Roman still in love with that high school Latin teacher
Taking her to that gymnasium again
    where the modest upright stood
Playing for her   trills and dissonance
        of a piano piece called, "Ruinae"
                ruins, plural

I don't know if Florence ever was a topic in her class
Or better, Firenze   the Italian

But she was keen to teach the grammar
And we *liked* Miss Darby
    and the dead language
        and not having to converse in it
        keeping it a strangely virgin tongue
            for all of Virgil and the rest of them
Staying distant from the Latin
Getting *close* to the Latin *teacher*

Florence is soon transcending
    the circumstance
    of being an American village
It says, "We're happy to have you!
      just know we are not a European destination"

And the history's somewhat shallow
Suitable for Valentines   and the concept "hunk of love"

Call it Firenze if you want
Right this minute   that's about all
Oh!   *except* for thinking north is south!

      that somehow directions have switched
      and the "bay" on the left is really the Pacific

Instead of south   it's back north you go
    hurriedly
    and the issue isn't quickly resolved

Half-asleep, something happened
A pivoting
    Harry again   a homing instinct
   "*do return*"
    so quickly you overshoot
       and find Alaska's doorstep

For the ride's reversed
    with inexplicable suddenness
    with no recollection of a pit stop's disorientation
     any reason for confusion
     what might have led to it

There was no gas
There were no groceries
There is only a return in progress
      and no one to ask for a second opinion

"Where's the west?"
    I'm going a wrong way that's really right
    and a fitting befuddlement
The many mirrors of deception polished

But what did you expect?!
Driving the coast road at night
    simultaneous journeys are completed
      two destinations decided
A long time passing
    the way divided attention allows that
    and is an enjoyable quandary

On either side   the sea
    like the mysteries of Franck
      whose *Beatitudes* still sound
     a chorus hushed   uncertainty abounding

A musical biography
A cat's gaze   the Orick cat involved
Yes, it's still the Palm Motel
    the mother cat
        rehearsing and rehearsing her sorcery

How *long* have I been going the wrong way?
    an hour?   all night?   all right!
Such an exquisite limbo not knowing
        and actually believing north is south
      all along   the dunes in the dark
        take a refresher course in reading maps

The sea rocks called The Sisters
Those are the difficult goal
We'll sleep there
    buffeted   cocooned
    like a chrysallis
Safe in safety from the clockwork inevitable

3 a.m. a not-unreasonable ETA
Establish south again
    retracing the route for anything familiar
      no   no   there is nothing

All along the dunes in the dark
It is Harry I think of
    and what he'd make of this messy exodus
    account paid in full to chaos theory

There was plenty of time to arrive the bluff
Hear the stories told by daylight or evening
                to a remembered moon

Actually   it's a *very* familiar place
At one time I'd made much of its elephant stone
    had taken others to see the hidden cavern
        in the wreckage of a fallen ceiling
And we'd studied the ocean's captured breakers
    where they finish   enclosed
    without consequence

They're always doing this
Defining perpetual motion
    in the heart of the elephant
        planning what's ahead
           while everything behind approaches

It's been morning
Since before the impressive automobile was sequestered
    nosed into the deep puddles of parking
        exhausted as myself
           craving disuse and abandonment

There was a ceremony
Wearing the jacket that cures you of pneumonia
    the warm one

Stones were returned that had been taken
Taken before   on a melancholy occasion
From these landslides' slopes
    they were pitched far   sightless
    arcing out just prior to bedtime
                it had to be done

I brought a sister back with that toss
    effortless   Karen and her critical faculties
What was the thought she'd ever departed?

The heart and the soul both underemployed
    while the day that was the night should last
    and a radio played
        the only station a static evocation

A promise of free miles, perhaps
The only station was good enough for approximate joy
    reviving in the presence of fortresses
Counting silently the separate castles
Remembering each address
    their endless shadows' ministrations

  At 3 a.m., yes   settle in at last
  Prepared for any cue   and additional dialogue

      motionless
          for the first time in eleven hours

And the morning *light*
    when it comes
    will be the overexposed frames
              of a prolonged denouement
              colliding with Sunday
     to rave reviews
    worthy of an Oscar nomination

The Sisters slept
I slept   slept trucker dreams
        alarmed against thievery

Dreams that told stories
     of bad behavior forgiven
        of sisters and brothers reconciled
That find out truth the old-fashioned way
While the subconscious instructs
           the tenets of philosophy relaxed

That dawn   pale
    like the moon making up
     for having only been a *theory* of moonlight
      and so overcompensating
     a financing involved

The radio was still alive
On waking   the mountain called Humbug couldn't be seen
   not really

Oh, there was a mountain all right!
    but it wasn't the one we counted on
    wasn't the geography   the map
It was *absentee*
    and the substitute stood
       suspicious in the haze up north

Overnight was the coast replaced
    and even the great monoliths demand explanation
     new geologic arguments

They are seen   nameless
     their proper names lost like a sibling
         she is unaccounted for   and formless

I'm a spy on the bluff
Trying to make sense of solid rock
         when only her spirit could do this
         lend animation

The seascape's friendly
     yet weakened with animus
         and first job jitters

Get in touch
Whichever rocks they are
     the scene is stagey
         homey despite the absence of a family
And I've been playing the fool
     imagining the coast has the power
         to summon second chances

Let us talk to an expert in the field
Someone else who drives to the Sisters
         from the far side of sanity
Who also waits in the pellucid morning
     for a sign from Neptune

"You've done enough"

The elephant advises it's not a rehearsal
I hear his bellowing above the surf sound
It's possible to fix the time
     ten o'clock   ante-meridian
     and a date in November
     the saddest month
         make it the seventeenth
In the year of our melanizing   2013

Enough of the twenty-first century lived already
     to dispense with the rest of it
     with formalities

If I told you what a morning it was
Absurdly greenbacked   even money-marketed
How the practical slid into fantasy
     in such a way it seemed a brush with the law

It will take years past extinction
     to parse what is before us
Fresh   as if nothing happened
To Harry
     to Gary
          to Karen
              to Orrin
                   to wives and husbands

Though California's still a distant border
     the film will here conclude

The film is broken and burns in the sprockets
Celluloid's hole expanding
     to be a screen so white
         it is the tumult of breakers

The edge   and finish   of motions of the ocean

www.ingramcontent.com/pod-product-compliance
Lightning Source LLC
Chambersburg PA
CBHW081430070526
44586CB00020B/2537